Numerology Step by Step

A Practical Approach to Numerology & Number Interpretation

Faith Phillips

© 2024 by Faith Phillips

All rights reserved.

No part of this publication may be reproduced, distributed, or transmitted in any form or by any means, including photocopying, recording, or other electronic or mechanical methods, without the prior written permission of the publisher, except for brief quotations in critical reviews and some other noncommercial uses permitted by copyright law.

This book is designed to provide general information regarding the topics discussed. It is offered with the understanding that neither the author nor the publisher is engaged in rendering financial, legal, or other professional advice. While efforts have been made to ensure the accuracy and reliability of the information contained in this publication, the author and publisher do not guarantee its accuracy or completeness and shall not be responsible for any errors, omissions, or for the results obtained from the use of such information. The material in this book is provided "as is," without any express or implied warranties.

Readers are encouraged to consult a qualified professional for advice tailored to their personal or professional situation. The strategies and information discussed may not be appropriate for every situation and are not promised or guaranteed to produce specific outcomes. Neither the author nor the publisher will be liable for any loss, damage, or other consequences that may arise from the use of or reliance on the information provided.

No representation is made about the quality of information provided exceeding that obtainable through professional advice. In no event will the author or publisher be responsible for any direct, indirect, incidental, consequential, or other damages resulting from the use of the information in this book.

PREFACE

Welcome to the study of Numerology! If you're curious about the hidden meanings behind the numbers in your life, you've come to the right place. This book, "Numerology Step by Step: A Practical Approach to Numerology & Number Interpretation," is your guide to unlocking the secrets of this ancient art.

Numerology has been studied and practiced for centuries, with roots tracing back to ancient civilizations. It is the study of the occult significance of numbers and their influence on our lives. Whether you're a complete beginner or someone with some experience in numerology, this book will take you on a journey of self-discovery and personal growth.

In these pages, you'll learn the core principles of numerology and how to apply them to your everyday life. We'll explore the history of this fascinating subject, debunk common myths, and go into the different types of numerology systems. You'll discover the importance of your personal numbers, from your Life Path to your Soul Urge, and learn how to calculate them with ease.

But this book is more than just a reference guide – it's a practical tool for personal transformation. By understanding the deeper meanings behind the numbers in your life, you'll gain insights into your personality, your relationships, your career, and your overall well-being. You'll learn how to use numerology to make informed decisions, overcome challenges, and align your life with your true purpose.

Throughout the book, you'll find real-life examples and case studies to illustrate the power of numerology in action. Whether you're looking to improve your romantic relationships, find your dream job, or simply gain a better understanding of yourself, this book will provide you with the knowledge and tools you need to succeed.

What sets this book apart is its step-by-step approach, making it accessible to readers of all backgrounds and experience levels. Each chapter builds upon the last, guiding you through the various aspects of numerology with clarity and precision. From calculating your core numbers to exploring advanced techniques, you'll have everything you need to start your numerology journey with confidence.

At the same time, each chapter and section is built to stand on its own for those prefer to pick and choose what to read, which means you might see some mild repetition here and there.

So, are you ready to unlock the hidden meanings in your life? Grab a pen and paper, and let's dive into the study of Numerology Step by Step. Get ready to discover the power of numbers and how they can transform your life in ways you never imagined.

TOPICAL OUTLINE

Chapter 1: Introduction to Numerology
- History of Numerology
- The Core Principles of Numerology
- The Significance of Numbers in Everyday Life
- The Different Types of Numerology Systems
- The Relationship Between Numerology and Astrology
- Common Myths and Misconceptions about Numerology
- The Importance of Personal Numbers
- How to Calculate Your Core Numbers
- Introduction to Master Numbers
- Numerology as a Tool for Personal Growth

Chapter 2: Life Path Numbers
- Calculating Your Life Path Number
- The Meanings of Each Life Path Number (1-9)
- Master Life Path Numbers (11, 22, 33)
- Interpreting Your Life Path in Daily Life

Chapter 3: Expression and Destiny Numbers
- Finding Your Expression Number
- The Significance of Destiny Numbers
- How Expression and Destiny Numbers Influence Your Life
- Compatibility of Expression Numbers with Other Core Numbers
- Expression Numbers in Personal and Professional Relationships (Examples)

Chapter 4: Soul Urge Numbers
- What is a Soul Urge Number?
- Discovering Your Soul Urge Number
- How Soul Urge Influences Your Desires and Motivations
- Aligning Your Life with Your Soul Urge

Chapter 5: Personality Numbers
- Understanding Personality Numbers
- Calculating Your Personality Number
- How Personality Numbers Shape First Impressions
- Balancing Personality with Other Core Numbers

Chapter 6: Birth Day Numbers
- The Importance of Your Birth Day Number
- How to Calculate Your Birth Day Number

- The Influence of Birth Day Numbers on Personal Traits
- Using Birth Day Numbers to Enhance Life Decisions
- Birth Day Numbers and Life Events

Chapter 7: Personal Year Numbers
- Introduction to Personal Year Cycles
- How to Determine Your Personal Year Number
- Understanding the Nine-Year Cycle in Numerology
- How Personal Year Numbers Affect Life Phases

Chapter 8: Pinnacle Numbers
- What are Pinnacle Numbers?
- Calculating Your Pinnacle Numbers
- The Four Pinnacle Phases in Life
- Using Pinnacle Numbers for Long-Term Planning

Chapter 9: Challenge Numbers
- Understanding Challenge Numbers
- How to Calculate Your Challenge Numbers
- Interpreting the Impact of Challenge Numbers
- Strategies for Overcoming Challenges in Numerology

Chapter 10: Karmic Numbers
- Introduction to Karmic Debt Numbers
- The Significance of Karmic Lessons
- Identifying Karmic Numbers in Your Chart
- How to Address and Balance Karmic Debt

Chapter 11: Master Numbers
- Interpreting Master Numbers 11, 22, and 33
- The Higher Vibration and Challenges of Master Numbers
- Incorporating Master Numbers into Daily Life
- Master Numbers in Spiritual Development

Chapter 12: Compatibility and Relationships in Numerology
- Numerology and Relationship Compatibility
- Comparing Life Path Numbers for Relationship Insights
- The Role of Destiny and Soul Urge Numbers in Relationships
- How Numerology Can Improve Communication and Harmony

Chapter 13: Numerology in Career and Finances
- Using Numerology to Choose a Career Path
- How Expression and Personality Numbers Influence Career Success
- The Role of Personal Year Numbers in Financial Planning

- Numerology for Wealth and Abundance

Chapter 14: Numerology and Health
- Understanding the Connection Between Numbers and Health
- How Life Path and Soul Urge Numbers Affect Well-being
- Identifying Health Challenges Through Numerology
- Using Numerology for Preventive Health Strategies

Chapter 15: Advanced Numerology Techniques
- Introduction to Name Numerology
- The Power of Changing Your Name
- Addressing Complex Numerology Charts
- Exploring the Numerology of Addresses and Locations
- Numerology and Business Naming

Chapter 16: Practical Applications of Numerology
- Numerology for Daily Decision Making
- Using Numerology for Personal and Spiritual Growth
- How to Interpret Recurring Numbers in Your Life
- Combining Numerology with Other Metaphysical Practices
- Developing Your Own Numerology Practice

Chapter 17: Historical Timeline of Numerology
- Timeline of Numerology

Appendix
- Terms and Definitions

Afterword

TABLE OF CONTENTS

Chapter 1: Introduction to Numerology ... 1
Chapter 2: Life Path Numbers ... 15
Chapter 3: Expression and Destiny Numbers ... 21
Chapter 4: Soul Urge Numbers ... 29
Chapter 5: Personality Numbers ... 34
Chapter 6: Birth Day Numbers ... 40
Chapter 7: Personal Year Numbers ... 47
Chapter 8: Pinnacle Numbers ... 53
Chapter 9: Challenge Numbers ... 58
Chapter 10: Karmic Numbers ... 64
Chapter 11: Master Numbers ... 70
Chapter 12: Compatibility and Relationships in Numerology ... 76
Chapter 13: Numerology in Career and Finances ... 82
Chapter 14: Numerology and Health ... 87
Chapter 15: Advanced Numerology Techniques ... 92
Chapter 16: Practical Applications of Numerology ... 102
Chapter 17: Historical Timeline of Numerology ... 111
Appendix ... 122
Afterword ... 126

CHAPTER 1: INTRODUCTION TO NUMEROLOGY

History of Numerology

Numerology traces its origins back thousands of years, emerging from the desire to understand the universe through numbers. The roots of numerology are often linked to ancient civilizations that observed patterns and cycles in nature. These early thinkers didn't just use numbers for counting; they saw numbers as symbols with profound meaning.

The Babylonians were among the first to assign significance to numbers. They lived around 5,000 years ago and are known for developing one of the earliest numerical systems. They believed that numbers had mystical properties and used them in divination. This wasn't just about predicting the future; they sought to understand the hidden forces that govern reality. Each number was thought to carry a specific vibration, influencing events and human behavior.

In ancient Egypt, numbers held a sacred status. The Egyptians used numbers not only in their architectural marvels like the pyramids but also in spiritual contexts. They associated numbers with their gods and goddesses, believing that these divine beings communicated through numerical signs. For example, the number 3 symbolized the heavens, while the number 2 represented duality, a concept central to their religious beliefs.

The most significant early development in numerology occurred in ancient Greece. **Pythagoras**, a philosopher and mathematician who lived around 570 to 495 BCE, is often credited as the father of modern numerology. Pythagoras founded a school that studied numbers not just as mathematical entities but as spiritual symbols. He believed that everything in the universe could be reduced to numbers and that each number had its own personality and attributes. His famous quote, "All is number," reflects this belief.

Pythagoras and his followers, known as the Pythagoreans, explored how numbers related to each other and to the natural world. They were particularly interested in the concept of harmony and balance, which they believed could be expressed through numerical relationships. For instance, they saw the number 10 as perfect because it is the sum of the first four digits (1+2+3+4), symbolizing wholeness and completeness. **The Pythagorean system** laid the foundation for much of the numerology practiced today.

As numerology spread, it evolved and adapted to different cultures. In China, numbers were deeply integrated into daily life through systems like **I Ching** and **feng shui**. The Chinese believed that numbers had both positive and negative energies, influencing everything from the success of a business to the health of an individual. The number 8, for instance, was considered extremely lucky because it sounds like the word for wealth in Chinese.

In India, numerology took shape through the **Vedas**, ancient sacred texts that included extensive numerical symbolism. Numbers were associated with planets and deities, and they were believed to influence an individual's life path. The number 9, representing the planet Mars, was seen as a powerful and dynamic force, bringing both strength and challenges.

During the Renaissance, interest in numerology surged once again in Europe. Scholars began revisiting ancient texts and Pythagorean theories, seeking to connect numbers with the divine. **Alchemy**, a precursor to modern chemistry, also incorporated numerological ideas, with alchemists using numbers in their attempts to transform base metals into gold and discover the elixir of life.

By the 19th and early 20th centuries, numerology had taken a more structured form. **L. Dow Balliett**, an American author, was instrumental in popularizing numerology in the United States. She combined Pythagorean teachings with Biblical references, arguing that numbers were key to understanding one's destiny. Balliett's work inspired others, like **Dr. Juno Jordan**, who developed the **Numerology of the Birth Force** method. This system analyzed the significance of birth dates and names, a practice that continues to be widely used in numerology today.

Modern numerology is a blend of these ancient traditions, refined and adapted over millennia. The core idea remains that numbers are more than just symbols for counting. They are believed to hold the key to understanding the universe and our place within it. Whether through the influence of Pythagorean thought or the mystical beliefs of ancient civilizations, numerology has persisted as a method for seeking meaning in the seemingly random events of life. This practice continues to evolve, drawing from both its rich history and the ongoing fascination with numbers.

The Core Principles of Numerology

Numerology is built on the idea that numbers are not just mathematical symbols but are imbued with unique vibrations that can influence various aspects of life. The core principles of numerology revolve around the understanding that each number holds a specific meaning, and these meanings can provide insights into personality, destiny, and the energies surrounding events. To comprehend numerology, it's essential to grasp these foundational principles.

The Life Path Number is perhaps the most significant number in numerology. It is derived from a person's birth date and is believed to reveal the path one is destined to follow in life. The Life Path Number is calculated by reducing the digits of the birth date to a single digit. For example, if someone was born on July 14, 1985, you would add 7 (July) + 1 + 4 (14th) + 1 + 9 + 8 + 5 (1985), which totals 35. Then, 3 + 5 = 8, making 8 the Life Path Number. Each number from 1 to 9 has distinct traits; in this case, 8 is associated with ambition, leadership, and material success.

Another fundamental principle is the **Expression or Destiny Number**, which is calculated from the letters of a person's full name. In numerology, each letter corresponds to a specific number (A=1, B=2, etc.). By adding these numbers together and reducing them to a single digit, you get the Destiny Number. This number is thought to represent the talents, strengths, and challenges that will manifest in one's life. For example, someone named "John Doe" would calculate the numbers for each letter (J=1, O=6, H=8, N=5; D=4, O=6, E=5). Adding them up gives 35, and reducing it gives 8. An 8 Destiny Number, similar to the Life Path Number, indicates a person driven by success and achievement.

The Soul Urge or Heart's Desire Number is another key element. It reflects a person's inner motivations, desires, and what they value most in life. This number is calculated using only the vowels in a person's name. For example, for "John Doe," the vowels are O (6) and E (5). Adding these gives 11, and 1+1 equals 2. A 2 Soul Urge Number suggests a deep need for harmony, partnership, and emotional connection.

The Personality Number is derived from the consonants in a person's name and reveals how others perceive them. It's often considered the outer layer of a person's character. For "John Doe," the consonants J (1), H (8), N (5), and D (4) would be added, totaling 18, which reduces to 9. A 9 Personality Number might indicate someone seen as compassionate, wise, and a bit mysterious.

Master Numbers (11, 22, 33) hold special significance in numerology and are not reduced to a single digit. These numbers are considered to carry higher vibrations and are linked to greater responsibilities and potential. For instance, 11 is often associated with intuition and spiritual insight, 22 with mastery and building, and 33 with the role of a teacher or healer.

The concept of cycles is also central to numerology. Life is viewed as a series of cycles, each governed by different numbers that influence the energies during specific periods. For example, the **Personal Year Number** is calculated by adding the digits of the birth day and month to the digits of the current year. This number provides insight into the themes and challenges one might face in a given year.

Through these principles, numerology provides a framework for understanding oneself and the world. Each number serves as a key to unlocking deeper meanings and patterns in life, offering guidance on how to navigate challenges, fulfill one's potential, and align with the natural flow of the universe.

The Significance of Numbers in Everyday Life

Numbers are more than mere tools for counting; they carry vibrations that subtly influence our daily lives. Numerology asserts that the numbers we encounter—whether in our birth date, name, or even addresses—hold significance that can impact our experiences and decisions. Understanding the significance of numbers in everyday life opens a window into how we interact with the world around us.

One of the most immediate ways numbers influence daily life is through the **Personal Day Number**. This number is calculated by adding the digits of the current date to your Personal Year Number. For example, if today's date is April 3, 2024, and your Personal Year Number is 6, you would add 4 (April) + 3 (3rd day) + 6 (Personal Year) = 13, which reduces to 4. A Personal Day Number of 4 might indicate a day best suited for organization, planning, and attending to details. By understanding your Personal Day Number, you can align your activities with the natural energy of the day, potentially making your efforts more effective.

House numbers are another example where numerology plays a role. The number of your home can influence the atmosphere and experiences you have there. If you live at 1234 Elm Street, you would add 1+2+3+4, which equals 10, and then reduce it to 1. A house with the number 1 might foster independence and innovation, making it ideal for someone who values autonomy and new beginnings. On the other hand, a house with the number 6 might be more nurturing and family-oriented, encouraging a warm, harmonious environment.

Numbers also appear in relationships. The **Relationship Compatibility Number** is found by comparing the Life Path Numbers of two individuals. If one person has a Life Path Number of 4 and the other has a 7, their relationship might be characterized by a balance between practicality (4) and introspection (7). Understanding these numbers can help couples appreciate their differences and work together more harmoniously.

Even mundane aspects of life, such as phone numbers or license plates, are believed to carry certain vibrations. A phone number that reduces to the number 3 might suggest communication, creativity, and social interactions. This might be particularly beneficial for someone in a profession where these qualities are important, such as a marketer or entertainer.

The significance of numbers extends to financial decisions as well. For instance, choosing a significant date for launching a business or making a major purchase can be guided by numerology. A date that reduces to the number 8 might be particularly auspicious for financial success, as 8 is associated with wealth, power, and material abundance. Business owners might look for an address with a favorable number or schedule important meetings on days that align with positive numerological vibrations.

In daily life, numerology can also guide personal development. Knowing your Life Path or Destiny Numbers can help you make decisions that align with your strengths and life purpose. If your Life Path Number is 3, you might find fulfillment in creative pursuits and should seek opportunities that allow you to express your ideas. On the other hand, if your Destiny Number is 9, you might be drawn to humanitarian efforts and find satisfaction in helping others.

Even the simple act of noticing recurring numbers in your life can be meaningful. Seeing the same number repeatedly, such as 11:11 on a clock, might be interpreted as a sign or message. Many believe that these recurring numbers are a form of communication from the universe, offering guidance or reassurance.

Incorporating numerology into everyday life allows for a deeper connection to the energies that shape our experiences. By paying attention to the numbers that surround us, we can gain insights into the patterns of our lives and make more informed choices that resonate with our true nature.

The Different Types of Numerology Systems

Numerology, the study of numbers and their mystical significance, has taken various forms around the world. While the core idea remains that numbers hold deeper meanings, different cultures have developed unique systems to explore these meanings. Each system offers its own perspective on how numbers influence our lives.

Pythagorean Numerology is perhaps the most widely known and practiced system today. Named after the ancient Greek philosopher Pythagoras, this system assigns numerical values to the letters of the alphabet (A=1, B=2, C=3, and so on) and focuses on reducing numbers to a single digit or master number (11, 22, 33). Pythagorean numerology is often used to calculate the Life Path Number, Destiny Number, and Soul Urge Number, each providing insights into different aspects of a person's character and destiny. For example, if someone's name is "Sarah," you would assign S=1, A=1, R=9, A=1, H=8, and then sum these numbers to get 20, which reduces to 2. In this system, the number 2 is associated with cooperation, balance, and sensitivity.

Chaldean Numerology is an older system originating from ancient Babylon. Unlike Pythagorean numerology, Chaldean numerology assigns numbers based on the vibration of each letter, rather than its order in the alphabet. In this system, the number values range from 1 to 8, with no letter assigned the number 9, as 9 is considered a sacred number. The focus in Chaldean numerology is often on the name, with the numbers offering insight into one's personality and the vibrations that influence their life. For instance, the name "Sarah" would be calculated as S=3, A=1, R=2, A=1, H=5, which totals 12, and reduces to 3. The number 3 in Chaldean numerology is linked to creativity, expression, and social interaction.

Kabbalistic Numerology has its roots in Jewish mysticism, specifically the Kabbalah. This system is deeply spiritual, focusing on the Hebrew alphabet, where each letter is associated with a specific number. The numbers derived from Kabbalistic numerology are believed to reveal the hidden, spiritual truths behind a person's name and life path. Unlike other systems, Kabbalistic numerology does not always reduce numbers to a single digit, as the specific number's original form carries unique significance. For example, the Hebrew letter Aleph (א) corresponds to the number 1, signifying unity and the beginning of all things. The calculations are often more complex, reflecting the intricate spiritual concepts within the Kabbalah.

Chinese Numerology is another system with deep cultural significance. In China, numbers are associated with both positive and negative energies based on their phonetic similarities to certain words. The number 8, for instance, is considered extremely lucky because it sounds like the word for prosperity. Conversely, the number 4 is often avoided because it sounds like the word for death. Chinese numerology also includes systems like the I Ching, where numbers have a key part in divination and understanding the flow of energy in the universe. A house with the number 8 in its address is often more desirable in Chinese culture because it is believed to attract wealth and good fortune.

Indian Numerology is closely linked to Vedic traditions and often incorporates elements of astrology. In Indian numerology, each number is associated with a planet, and these planetary influences are considered when interpreting the numbers. The number 9, for example, is ruled by Mars and is seen as powerful and dynamic, often associated with leadership and courage. Names and birth dates are analyzed to understand a person's karma and life purpose. For instance, if someone's name number is 9, they might be seen as having a strong, assertive personality, influenced by the energy of Mars.

Japanese Numerology includes practices such as "Ketsu," which is the analysis of numbers in relation to blood types and personality traits. Although less well-known globally, Japanese numerology blends numbers with traditional beliefs about health, personality, and destiny. A person's birth date and blood type might be analyzed to offer insights into their future and well-being.

These different numerology systems reflect the diverse ways in which cultures have sought to understand the world through numbers. Each system offers unique insights, shaped by the cultural, spiritual, and philosophical contexts in which they developed. Whether you follow the Pythagorean system, delve into Chaldean calculations, or explore the spiritual depth of Kabbalistic numerology, the common thread is the belief that numbers are not just mathematical constructs but keys to understanding the deeper aspects of life.

The Relationship Between Numerology and Astrology

Numerology and astrology are two ancient practices that both seek to understand human life and the universe by exploring the connections between numbers, celestial bodies, and human experiences. Though distinct, these disciplines often overlap, with many practitioners using them in tandem to gain deeper insights into personality, destiny, and life events.

At the heart of both numerology and astrology is the idea that everything in the universe is interconnected. Numerology uses numbers to uncover hidden meanings and patterns in our lives, while astrology uses the positions and movements of celestial bodies to do the same. **Both systems are rooted in the concept of cosmic energy**—that the universe operates on a set of vibrations and frequencies that influence all living things.

One of the most direct relationships between numerology and astrology is through the **Life Path Number** in numerology and the **Sun Sign** in astrology. The Life Path Number, derived from a person's birth date, is considered a reflection of their core identity and life purpose, much like the Sun Sign in astrology, which is determined by the position of the sun at the time of one's birth. For example, someone with a Life Path Number of 5 might be adventurous and free-spirited, similar to how a Sagittarius Sun Sign is often characterized by a love for exploration and new experiences.

Astrology also associates numbers with specific celestial bodies. For example, in both Western astrology and numerology, the number 3 is linked to Jupiter, the planet of expansion, optimism, and abundance. In numerology, a person with a strong influence of the number 3 might be seen as creative and expressive, traits often attributed to Jupiter's expansive nature in astrology. Similarly, the number 8 is associated with Saturn, representing discipline, structure, and responsibility, both in astrological terms and numerological interpretations.

Another area where numerology and astrology intersect is in the calculation of **Personal Year Numbers** and **Personalized Astrological Forecasts**. Both methods provide a way to understand the energies influencing an individual during a specific period. In numerology, a Personal Year Number is calculated by adding the digits of the current year to your birth date, revealing the themes and challenges of that year. In astrology, transits and progressions show how the movement of planets will affect different areas of your life in the coming year. For instance, a Personal Year Number of 4 suggests a year of hard work and building foundations, which might align with a significant Saturn transit in your astrological chart, emphasizing the need for discipline and focus.

Astrological houses also have numerical significance that can be related to numerology. The astrological chart is divided into 12 houses, each representing different areas of life, from self-identity (1st house) to dreams and spirituality (12th house). In numerology, these houses can be explored through the numbers 1 to 12, with each number bringing its own meaning. For example, the 7th house in astrology is associated with partnerships and is often linked with the number 7 in numerology, which symbolizes introspection and spiritual connections. Understanding how these numbers align can offer deeper insights into one's relationships and partnerships.

In addition, **the concept of cycles** is central to both numerology and astrology. Just as numerology explores cycles through Personal Year Numbers, astrology examines cycles through the orbits of planets, particularly Saturn (around 29.5 years) and Jupiter (around 12 years). Both disciplines recognize that life progresses through phases and that understanding these cycles can help us navigate challenges and make the most of opportunities.

The relationship between numerology and astrology extends beyond mere similarities; they complement each other, offering a fuller picture of the forces at play in an individual's life. For those who study or practice both, numerology can provide additional layers of meaning to astrological interpretations, and vice versa. Whether you are interpreting a Life Path Number or examining your astrological chart, these systems together create a more comprehensive toolset for understanding the mysteries of existence and guiding personal growth.

Common Myths and Misconceptions about Numerology

Numerology, like many esoteric practices, is surrounded by myths and misconceptions that can obscure its true purpose and meaning. These misunderstandings often stem from a lack of knowledge or from oversimplifications that spread through popular culture. It's essential to address these myths to appreciate what numerology truly offers.

Myth 1: Numerology is Just a Superstition

One of the most common misconceptions is that numerology is mere superstition, akin to avoiding black cats or walking under ladders. While numerology does involve a belief in the mystical significance of numbers, it is far from a baseless superstition. Numerology is grounded in centuries of philosophical thought, particularly Pythagorean principles, which suggest that numbers are a universal language with deep connections to the patterns of life. For instance, Pythagoras, a respected mathematician, and philosopher, believed that numbers were the essence of all things. Numerology uses numbers to uncover these underlying truths, offering insights into personality, life paths, and the nature of existence itself.

Myth 2: Numerology Can Predict the Future with Certainty

Another widespread myth is that numerology can predict the future with absolute accuracy. While numerology can provide guidance and reveal potential trends, it does not offer precise predictions. Instead, it is a tool for understanding the energies and influences that may shape future events. For example, if your Personal Year Number suggests a period of change, numerology can help you prepare and make informed decisions. However, it does not guarantee specific outcomes. Numerology emphasizes free will; it is not about fate being set in stone but about understanding the potentials and challenges ahead.

Myth 3: Numerology Is Based Solely on Western Practices

Many people assume that numerology is exclusively a Western practice, often only associated with Pythagoras and the Greek tradition. However, numerology has roots in various cultures worldwide. For example, Chaldean numerology originates from ancient Babylon, while Chinese numerology incorporates elements of feng shui and the I Ching. Indian numerology aligns with Vedic astrology and is deeply ingrained in the spiritual practices of the region. Each system offers unique insights, demonstrating that numerology is a global phenomenon with diverse applications and interpretations.

Myth 4: Numerology Is a Religion

Some believe that numerology is a religious practice or that it conflicts with religious beliefs. In reality, numerology is not a religion; it does not involve worship, dogma, or rituals. Instead, it is a system of knowledge that can complement religious or spiritual practices. Many people of various faiths use numerology as a tool for self-discovery and understanding the world around them. For example, some Christians use numerology to explore the significance of numbers in the Bible, while others might use it to enhance their meditation practices. Numerology is versatile and can be adapted to fit different belief systems.

Myth 5: Numerology Is Only About Positive Predictions

Another misconception is that numerology always delivers good news. While numerology can highlight strengths and opportunities, it also points out challenges and potential pitfalls. For instance, a Life Path Number might reveal that someone is prone to overconfidence or indecision, urging them to be mindful of these tendencies. Numerology provides a balanced view, offering both encouragement and caution, depending on the numbers involved. This balanced perspective is crucial for personal growth and self-awareness.

Understanding these myths and misconceptions helps to clarify what numerology truly is: a tool for gaining insight into the self and the world, rather than a rigid or mystical belief system. By dispelling these misunderstandings, individuals can approach numerology with an open mind and use it to enhance their personal and spiritual development.

The Importance of Personal Numbers

In numerology, personal numbers are seen as keys to understanding oneself, offering insights into personality, life purpose, and the challenges one might face. These numbers are derived from an individual's name and birth date, and each one carries a unique vibration that influences various aspects of life. Understanding and working with these personal numbers can be a powerful tool for self-discovery and personal growth.

Life Path Number is often considered the most critical personal number in numerology. It is calculated by adding the digits of one's birth date and reducing them to a single digit (unless it's a master number like 11, 22, or 33). This number reveals the core of who you are, your purpose in life, and the lessons you are meant to learn. For instance, someone with a Life Path Number 1 is likely to be a natural leader, independent and driven by a desire to achieve. In contrast, a Life Path Number 7 might indicate a person who is introspective, spiritual, and drawn to seeking deeper truths. Understanding your Life Path Number helps you align with your true purpose and navigate life's challenges more effectively.

The Destiny Number (or Expression Number) is another significant personal number, derived from the full name given at birth. This number represents your potential, talents, and what you are destined to accomplish in this lifetime. For example, if your Destiny Number is 4, you might excel in fields requiring organization, discipline, and hard work. You could find satisfaction in building systems or creating stability, both for yourself and others. Knowing your Destiny Number can guide you in making career choices or pursuing hobbies that resonate with your innate abilities.

The Soul Urge Number (or Heart's Desire Number) reflects your innermost desires, what truly motivates you, and what you need to feel fulfilled. This number is calculated by summing the values of the vowels in your full name. For example, if your Soul Urge Number is 6, you likely have a deep desire for harmony, love, and nurturing relationships. You might feel most content when you are caring for others or creating a peaceful home environment. Understanding this number helps you identify what you need to pursue to achieve inner peace and satisfaction.

The Personality Number is derived from the consonants in your name and reveals how others perceive you. It's the outer layer of your personality, the traits that are most visible to others. For instance, a Personality Number 3 might indicate someone who is seen as outgoing, expressive, and creative. This number can be particularly useful in understanding how you come across in social or professional settings, allowing you to make adjustments if necessary to align with your true self.

The Birth Day Number, the day of the month you were born, also carries special significance. It provides insight into a particular talent or ability that is innate to you. For example, someone born on the 14th might have a natural talent for communication and a love for learning, as the number 14 reduces to 5, which is associated with curiosity and versatility. This number can guide you in recognizing and developing these natural talents.

Personal Year Number is another essential number in numerology, calculated annually by adding the digits of the current year to your birth day and month. This number helps you understand the themes and energies that will dominate your life for that year. For example, if your Personal Year Number is 9, you might be in a period of completion, letting go of what no longer serves you, and preparing for new beginnings. Knowing your Personal Year Number can help you plan and set intentions that align with the year's energies.

Personal numbers in numerology serve as a map, guiding you through life's journey. They provide insights into your strengths, challenges, and the lessons you are meant to learn. By understanding and embracing these numbers, you can make more informed decisions, align with your true purpose, and ultimately, live a more fulfilling life.

How to Calculate Your Core Numbers

Calculating your core numbers in numerology involves simple mathematical steps based on your birth date and full name at birth. These core numbers provide insights into your personality, life path, and destiny, each offering a unique perspective on your life's journey.

Life Path Number is the most crucial number in numerology. To calculate it, add together the digits of your birth date. For example, if you were born on July 14, 1985, you would calculate as follows: 7 (for July) + 1 + 4 (day of birth) + 1 + 9 + 8 + 5 (year of birth). This gives a total of 35. You then reduce 35 to a single digit by adding 3 + 5, resulting in 8. Thus, your Life Path Number is 8, which signifies ambition, leadership, and material success.

The Expression Number (also known as the Destiny Number) is calculated from the full name given at birth. Each letter in your name is assigned a number based on its position in the alphabet (A=1, B=2, C=3, and so on). Add up these numbers for each letter in your name, and then reduce the sum to a single digit. For instance, if your name is "John Doe," J=1, O=6, H=8, N=5, D=4, O=6, E=5. Adding these together gives 35, which reduces to 8. The Expression Number 8 suggests that you are destined for roles that involve leadership, organization, and achievement.

The Soul Urge Number reflects your innermost desires and what drives you. To calculate it, use only the vowels in your full name. For example, in "John Doe," the vowels are O=6 and E=5. Adding these gives 11, and since 11 is a master number, it is not reduced further. A Soul Urge Number of 11 suggests a deep yearning for spiritual understanding and a desire to inspire others.

The Personality Number is derived from the consonants in your name. It reveals how others perceive you. Using "John Doe" again, the consonants are J=1, H=8, N=5, D=4, adding up to 18, which reduces to 9. A Personality Number 9 indicates that others see you as compassionate, wise, and perhaps a bit mysterious.

The Birth Day Number is simply the day of the month you were born, without any further reduction. For example, if you were born on the 14th, your Birth Day Number is 14, which is often associated with dynamic energy and a love for change and variety.

By understanding how to calculate these core numbers, you gain a personalized numerological profile that helps you understand your strengths, challenges, and life's purpose. These numbers form the foundation of numerology and provide insights into who you are and what you are meant to achieve in this lifetime.

Introduction to Master Numbers

Master Numbers in numerology are considered powerful and highly significant. Unlike other numbers, which are typically reduced to a single digit, Master Numbers —11, 22, and 33—are left in their double-digit form because they carry a unique vibration and potential. These numbers are believed to represent a higher level of spiritual awareness, responsibility, and mastery.

The Number 11 is often called the "Master Intuitive" or "Master Teacher." It is associated with spiritual insight, intuition, and enlightenment. Individuals with a Life Path or Destiny Number 11 are often highly sensitive and possess a deep understanding of the unseen forces in the world. They are drawn to helping others awaken to their spiritual truths. For example, someone with a Life Path Number 11 might feel compelled to pursue a career in healing, counseling, or teaching, where they can use their intuitive abilities to guide and support others.

The Number 22 is known as the "Master Builder." It is associated with the ability to turn dreams into reality through practical, tangible efforts. People with a Master Number 22 in their numerology chart are often visionaries who can achieve great things. They possess the unique ability to balance lofty ideals with practical action. For instance, a person with a Destiny Number 22 might excel in roles that involve large-scale projects, such as architecture, engineering, or leadership positions where they can implement grand visions with precision and efficiency.

The Number 33 is sometimes referred to as the "Master Healer" or "Master Teacher." It embodies the energies of compassion, love, and altruism. Those with a Master Number 33 are often called to serve humanity in profound ways, focusing on healing, teaching, or humanitarian efforts. A Life Path or Destiny Number 33 suggests a person who is deeply committed to helping others, often at a global scale. An example might be a person who dedicates their life to charitable work or becomes a spiritual leader, inspiring others through their selfless actions and teachings.

Master Numbers bring both great potential and significant challenges. The energy of these numbers is intense, and individuals with Master Numbers in their charts often face greater responsibilities and higher expectations. They are called to rise above personal concerns and focus on the broader impact they can have on the world. However, if not balanced, the intensity of Master Numbers can lead to feelings of overwhelm, anxiety, or a sense of being misunderstood.

In summary, Master Numbers 11, 22, and 33 represent heightened spiritual potential and responsibility. They offer unique opportunities for growth and contribution but also demand a greater level of self-awareness and dedication. Understanding these numbers can help individuals navigate the challenges they bring while fulfilling their higher purpose.

Numerology as a Tool for Personal Growth

Numerology serves as a framework for personal growth, offering insights into the self that can guide individuals on their journey of self-discovery and transformation. By understanding the significance of numbers in your life, you can uncover patterns, identify strengths and weaknesses, and make informed decisions that align with your true purpose.

One of the primary ways numerology fosters personal growth is through the **Life Path Number**. This number, derived from your birth date, reveals your core personality traits, challenges, and life's mission. For example, if your Life Path Number is 4, numerology suggests that you are likely disciplined, practical, and reliable. However, you might also struggle with rigidity and fear of change. By recognizing these traits, you can work on being more adaptable while leveraging your strengths in organization and stability to achieve your goals.

The Expression Number also is important in personal development. This number reflects your natural talents and the skills you are meant to develop in this lifetime. Understanding your Expression Number can help you choose a career path or hobbies that align with your inherent abilities, leading to greater fulfillment. For instance, if your Expression Number is 3, you are likely creative and expressive. You might find satisfaction in artistic endeavors, such as writing, painting, or performing, and numerology encourages you to nurture these talents.

Numerology also emphasizes the importance of understanding your challenges. The Karmic Debt Numbers (13, 14, 16, and 19) reveal lessons that you need to learn based on past actions. For example, if you have a Karmic Debt Number of 13, you might need to overcome laziness and embrace hard work and discipline. Acknowledging these challenges allows you to consciously work on them, transforming potential weaknesses into strengths.

Personal Year Numbers provide a yearly guide that helps you navigate the ebb and flow of life. Each year brings different energies, and knowing your Personal Year Number can help you align with these energies to make the most of your opportunities. For example, if you are in a Personal Year 5, numerology suggests that this is a year of change, adventure, and freedom. Understanding this can help you embrace new experiences and adapt to changes, knowing that this is a time for exploration and growth.

Numerology also encourages self-reflection and mindfulness, essential components of personal growth. By regularly consulting your numerology chart, you can gain a deeper understanding of your motivations, desires, and fears. This ongoing self-awareness helps you make choices that are in harmony with your true self, leading to a more authentic and fulfilling life.

Moreover, numerology can serve as a tool for improving relationships. By understanding the numerology charts of those close to you, you can gain insights into their personality traits, desires, and challenges. This knowledge fosters empathy and understanding, allowing for deeper and more harmonious connections.

In short, numerology offers a structured yet intuitive framework for personal growth. By exploring the numbers that influence your life, you can gain insights that guide you toward a path of self-improvement, fulfillment, and spiritual development. Whether through understanding your core traits, embracing your challenges, or navigating the cycles of life, numerology provides the tools to help you grow into your best self.

CHAPTER 2: LIFE PATH NUMBERS

Calculating Your Life Path Number

Calculating your Life Path Number is a fundamental step in understanding numerology. This number reveals essential insights into your personality, strengths, challenges, and the general direction of your life. It's straightforward to calculate, but the implications can be profound.

To begin, your Life Path Number is derived from your birth date. This is the number that most numerologists believe defines your core self—the essence of who you are and what you are meant to do in this lifetime. The process of calculating it involves reducing your full birth date to a single digit or, in some cases, a master number.

Let's walk through an example. Imagine someone born on July 14, 1985. To calculate their Life Path Number, start by breaking down the birth date into its components: the month, the day, and the year. In this case:

- The month of July is the 7th month, so it remains 7.
- The day of birth is 14. You reduce this by adding 1 + 4 to get 5.
- The year 1985 is broken down by adding the digits together: 1 + 9 + 8 + 5 = 23. You then reduce 23 by adding 2 + 3, which equals 5.

Now, add these three numbers together: 7 (for July) + 5 (for the 14th) + 5 (for 1985). This totals 17. You reduce this final number by adding 1 + 7, which equals 8. Thus, the Life Path Number for this birth date is 8.

It's important to note that there are exceptions in the reduction process. If during any stage of reduction you arrive at 11, 22, or 33, you do not reduce these numbers further. These are considered Master Numbers in numerology and carry a different, more intense vibration. For example, if your calculations resulted in 11 instead of 8, your Life Path Number would be 11, not 2. Master Numbers are seen as having higher spiritual significance, representing potentials for greater challenges and rewards.

Let's consider another example with a different birth date: December 29, 1974.

- December is the 12th month. Reducing this gives 1 + 2 = 3.
- The day, 29, is reduced by adding 2 + 9, which equals 11. Since 11 is a Master Number, it stays as 11.

- The year 1974 is reduced by adding 1 + 9 + 7 + 4, which equals 21, and then 2 + 1 = 3.

Adding these together gives 3 (for December) + 11 (for the 29th) + 3 (for 1974). This totals 17, and reducing 17 gives 1 + 7 = 8. In this case, the Life Path Number is 8.

However, if the total had been 11, 22, or 33 after the initial addition, you would stop there and recognize it as a Master Number rather than reducing further.

Life Path Numbers range from 1 to 9, with 11, 22, and 33 as Master Numbers. Each number carries its own set of characteristics:

- **1** represents independence, leadership, and innovation.
- **2** signifies diplomacy, sensitivity, and cooperation.
- **3** is associated with creativity, communication, and self-expression.
- **4** relates to practicality, organization, and building solid foundations.
- **5** embodies freedom, adventure, and adaptability.
- **6** stands for responsibility, care, and nurturing.
- **7** is linked to introspection, spirituality, and analytical thinking.
- **8** represents power, material success, and ambition.
- **9** signifies compassion, humanitarianism, and idealism.

Master Numbers carry these meanings at a heightened level:

- **11** involves spiritual insight, intuition, and enlightenment.
- **22** is the number of the Master Builder, combining vision with practical action.
- **33** is often called the Master Teacher, focusing on altruism and healing.

Understanding your Life Path Number gives you a clearer sense of direction and purpose. It serves as a guide to understanding why you encounter certain challenges and what strengths you can draw upon to overcome them. By recognizing the qualities and tendencies associated with your Life Path Number, you can align your actions more closely with your true self and navigate your life's journey with greater confidence.

The Meanings of Each Life Path Number (1-9)

In numerology, each Life Path Number from 1 to 9 carries distinct characteristics and themes that influence a person's life journey. Understanding the meaning behind your Life Path Number can provide insights into your personality, strengths, challenges, and overall life purpose.

Life Path 1 is associated with leadership, independence, and innovation. People with this number are natural leaders, often driven by a strong sense of self and a desire to achieve. They are pioneers who prefer to carve their own path rather than follow others. For example, someone with a Life Path 1 might excel in entrepreneurial endeavors or roles that require initiative and decision-making.

Life Path 2 signifies diplomacy, sensitivity, and cooperation. Those with this number are often peacemakers who excel in bringing people together and fostering harmony. They are empathetic, understanding, and adept at resolving conflicts. A Life Path 2 individual might find fulfillment in careers like counseling, mediation, or any role that requires tact and collaboration.

Life Path 3 is linked to creativity, communication, and self-expression. People with this number are often artistic and thrive in environments that allow them to express themselves freely. They are charismatic and social, with a natural ability to entertain and inspire others. Someone with a Life Path 3 might pursue careers in the arts, writing, or public speaking.

Life Path 4 relates to practicality, organization, and building solid foundations. Individuals with this number are disciplined, reliable, and focused on creating stability in their lives. They excel in roles that require attention to detail and a methodical approach. A Life Path 4 person might be drawn to careers in engineering, accounting, or any field that values structure and order.

Life Path 5 embodies freedom, adventure, and adaptability. Those with this number crave variety and are often restless in routine environments. They thrive on change and are always seeking new experiences. A Life Path 5 individual might excel in careers that involve travel, sales, or any role that allows for flexibility and exploration.

Life Path 6 stands for responsibility, care, and nurturing. People with this number are often drawn to helping others and creating a harmonious environment. They are compassionate and often take on roles that involve caring for others. Someone with a Life Path 6 might find fulfillment in teaching, healthcare, or social work.

Life Path 7 is linked to introspection, spirituality, and analytical thinking. Individuals with this number are seekers of truth, often drawn to the mysteries of life. They are introspective and prefer solitude to deep thinking and spiritual exploration. A Life Path 7 person might excel in research, philosophy, or any field that values deep analysis and understanding.

Life Path 8 represents power, material success, and ambition. Those with this number are driven to achieve and often find success in business or finance. They are natural leaders with a strong sense of purpose and the ability to execute their plans effectively. A Life Path 8 individual might pursue a career in management, entrepreneurship, or any role that involves leadership and financial acumen.

Life Path 9 signifies compassion, humanitarianism, and idealism. People with this number are often driven by a desire to make the world a better place. They are compassionate, selfless, and deeply concerned with the welfare of others. A Life Path 9 person might be drawn to careers in activism, charity work, or any field that involves service to others.

Master Life Path Numbers (11, 22, 33)

Master Life Path Numbers—11, 22, and 33—are considered to have higher vibrations and greater potential than other numbers. These numbers carry intense energy, representing both significant opportunities and challenges. They are seen as more demanding, often requiring individuals to fulfill a higher spiritual or social purpose.

Life Path 11 is known as the Master Intuitive or Master Teacher. It embodies spiritual insight, enlightenment, and an innate understanding of the deeper aspects of life. People with a Life Path 11 often possess heightened sensitivity and intuition, making them natural healers, counselors, or spiritual guides. However, the energy of 11 can also bring about intense emotions and challenges related to self-doubt or anxiety. For example, a person with Life Path 11 might feel a strong calling toward spiritual leadership but also experience periods of uncertainty about their path.

Life Path 22 is referred to as the Master Builder. It combines the visionary aspects of 11 with the practical abilities to manifest dreams into reality. Individuals with this number have the potential to achieve great things, particularly in building or creating something lasting and significant. They are often seen as architects of their environment, whether that be physical structures, businesses, or social systems. However, the pressure to succeed can be overwhelming. A Life Path 22 individual might excel in roles like engineering, architecture, or leadership positions that require both vision and execution.

Life Path 33 is called the Master Teacher or Master Healer. It is the number of universal love, compassion, and selfless service. People with a Life Path 33 are often driven by a desire to heal and help others on a large scale. They are idealists who want to bring love and light into the world, often through teaching, counseling, or humanitarian work. However, the energy of 33 can be challenging, as it demands a level of selflessness and dedication that can be difficult to sustain. A Life Path 33 person might be drawn to roles like spiritual leadership, social work, or any field where they can make a profound impact on others' lives.

Master Numbers offer the potential for extraordinary achievement but require a deep commitment to personal growth and the fulfillment of a higher purpose. Those with Master Numbers in their numerology charts are often called to go beyond personal concerns and contribute to the greater good, facing both great rewards and significant challenges along the way.

Interpreting Your Life Path in Daily Life

Understanding your Life Path Number in numerology can be a powerful tool for navigating daily life. This number provides insights into your core personality traits, strengths, and challenges, guiding you in making decisions that align with your true self. By integrating the knowledge of your Life Path Number into your everyday experiences, you can make choices that lead to a more fulfilling and purpose-driven life.

If your **Life Path Number is 1**, for example, you are naturally inclined toward leadership and independence. In your daily life, this might mean that you thrive in situations where you can take charge or initiate new projects. When faced with a decision, you might feel most comfortable when you have the autonomy to make choices on your terms. Recognizing this can help you seek out roles or opportunities where you can exercise your leadership skills, whether at work or in your personal life.

For those with a **Life Path Number 2**, harmony and cooperation are key themes. In daily interactions, you might find yourself acting as a mediator, seeking to resolve conflicts and bring people together. Understanding this can guide you in choosing environments that value teamwork and collaboration. When making decisions, consider how your actions will impact others and how you can contribute to a peaceful and balanced outcome.

A **Life Path Number 3** suggests a natural affinity for creativity and communication. In your daily life, you might feel most fulfilled when engaging in activities that allow you to express yourself, whether through writing, art, or social interactions. Recognizing this can help you prioritize opportunities that nurture your creative side, such as pursuing hobbies or careers that involve storytelling, design, or public speaking.

If your **Life Path Number is 4**, practicality and organization are your strengths. This might manifest in your daily life through a preference for routine and structure. You likely feel most at ease when your environment is orderly and your plans are well thought out. Embracing this can help you create systems that support your goals, whether that's through meticulous planning at work or maintaining a well-organized home.

For those with a **Life Path Number 5**, adventure and change are essential. In your daily life, you might find yourself drawn to new experiences and resistant to routine. Understanding this can help you seek out opportunities for travel, exploration, and learning. When making decisions, consider how you can incorporate variety and flexibility into your life, avoiding situations that feel overly restrictive or monotonous.

A **Life Path Number 6** is all about responsibility and care. In your daily life, you might be the one people turn to for support and guidance. Understanding this can help you embrace roles that involve nurturing others, whether in your family, community, or profession. When making decisions, consider how your actions can contribute to the well-being of those around you, as you likely find fulfillment in service and caregiving.

For those with a **Life Path Number 7**, introspection and spirituality are central themes. You might feel most comfortable when you have time for reflection and deep thought. Understanding this can help you carve out time for solitude and contemplation in your daily life. Whether through meditation, study, or quiet walks in nature, finding ways to connect with your inner self can be deeply fulfilling.

A **Life Path Number 8** is focused on power and achievement. In your daily life, you might be driven by goals and ambitions, seeking success in whatever you do. Recognizing this can help you set clear objectives and pursue them with determination. Whether in your career, finances, or personal projects, embracing your drive for success can lead to significant accomplishments.

For those with a **Life Path Number 9**, compassion and humanitarianism are guiding forces. In your daily life, you might be drawn to causes that involve helping others and making the world a better place. Understanding this can guide you toward volunteer work, advocacy, or any activities that allow you to contribute to society. When making decisions, consider how your actions can have a positive impact on the broader community.

By interpreting your Life Path Number in the context of daily life, you can make choices that resonate with your true self.

CHAPTER 3: EXPRESSION AND DESTINY NUMBERS

Finding Your Expression Number

Finding your Expression Number, also known as your Destiny Number, is a key step in understanding the path you are meant to follow in life. This number, derived from the letters in your full birth name, reveals your natural talents, abilities, and the opportunities that will present themselves as you progress through life. Unlike the Life Path Number, which is based on your birth date, the Expression Number focuses on your potential and the skills you are meant to develop.

To calculate your Expression Number, you need to assign a numerical value to each letter of your full birth name. In numerology, each letter corresponds to a number between 1 and 9:

- $A = 1, B = 2, C = 3, D = 4, E = 5, F = 6, G = 7, H = 8, I = 9$
- $J = 1, K = 2, L = 3, M = 4, N = 5, O = 6, P = 7, Q = 8, R = 9$
- $S = 1, T = 2, U = 3, V = 4, W = 5, X = 6, Y = 7, Z = 8$

Let's walk through an example. Imagine your full birth name is "Sophia Marie Johnson." To find your Expression Number, you'll first break down each part of the name:

- Sophia: $S = 1, O = 6, P = 7, H = 8, I = 9, A = 1$. Adding these together: $1 + 6 + 7 + 8 + 9 + 1 = 32$. Then reduce 32 by adding $3 + 2$, which equals 5.
- Marie: $M = 4, A = 1, R = 9, I = 9, E = 5$. Adding these together: $4 + 1 + 9 + 9 + 5 = 28$. Then reduce 28 by adding $2 + 8$, which equals 10, and reduce further to $1 + 0 = 1$.
- Johnson: $J = 1, O = 6, H = 8, N = 5, S = 1, O = 6, N = 5$. Adding these together: $1 + 6 + 8 + 5 + 1 + 6 + 5 = 32$. Then reduce 32 by adding $3 + 2$, which equals 5.

Now, you add the numbers from each name together: 5 (from Sophia) + 1 (from Marie) + 5 (from Johnson) = 11. In numerology, 11 is a Master Number, which means it carries a higher spiritual significance and is not reduced further. Therefore, the Expression Number for Sophia Marie Johnson is 11.

Master Numbers, like 11, 22, and 33, indicate that the person has a special potential for leadership, creativity, or spiritual growth. These numbers bring with them both higher challenges and higher rewards. For instance, someone with an

Expression Number 11 might find themselves naturally drawn to roles that require inspiration, intuition, and the ability to guide others.

If your name does not reduce to a Master Number, you would simply use the resulting single-digit number as your Expression Number. Each number from 1 to 9 has its own unique set of traits and potential:

- **1** suggests leadership, independence, and a pioneering spirit.
- **2** indicates diplomacy, cooperation, and a talent for bringing people together.
- **3** embodies creativity, communication, and the ability to inspire others.
- **4** is about practicality, organization, and building solid foundations.
- **5** reflects adaptability, freedom, and a love for adventure.
- **6** represents responsibility, care, and a nurturing nature.
- **7** is linked to introspection, analysis, and spiritual growth.
- **8** focuses on ambition, power, and material success.
- **9** signifies compassion, humanitarianism, and a global perspective.

Knowing your Expression Number provides insight into the skills and talents you are meant to develop throughout your life. For example, if your Expression Number is 3, you might find that opportunities for creative expression and communication are plentiful in your life. You may be naturally drawn to roles where you can use your voice or creativity to influence others, such as in the arts, media, or public speaking.

On the other hand, if your Expression Number is 8, you may have a natural affinity for business, finance, or leadership roles. You might feel a strong drive to achieve material success and influence, with opportunities arising in areas where you can manage resources, lead others, or build something of lasting value.

Understanding your Expression Number helps you recognize the path that aligns with your true self. It illuminates the qualities you possess and the areas where you can excel, guiding you toward a fulfilling and purpose-driven life. Whether you embrace leadership, creativity, or service, your Expression Number serves as a blueprint for realizing your full potential.

The Significance of Destiny Numbers

In numerology, the Destiny Number, also known as the Expression Number, is important in understanding your life's purpose and the path you are meant to follow. This number is derived from the full name given at birth and is believed to reveal your innate talents, abilities, and the potential you carry throughout your life. The Destiny Number is not about predicting the future but about understanding the qualities you were born with and how you can best use them to fulfill your life's mission.

Your Destiny Number reflects the opportunities and challenges you are likely to encounter as you move through life. It serves as a guide, helping you to recognize the areas where you naturally excel and the traits you should develop to achieve your fullest potential. For example, if your Destiny Number is 3, you are likely to be gifted in communication, creativity, and self-expression. This suggests that careers or activities involving writing, speaking, or the arts might be particularly fulfilling for you.

To find your Destiny Number, you assign a numerical value to each letter of your full birth name, using a system where A=1, B=2, C=3, and so on. You then add these numbers together and reduce them to a single digit, unless the number is a Master Number like 11, 22, or 33, which is not reduced further. Each resulting number carries specific traits and characteristics:

- **1** represents leadership, independence, and innovation. People with a Destiny Number 1 are often pioneers who are driven to create and lead.
- **2** signifies cooperation, diplomacy, and sensitivity. Those with this number excel in roles that require mediation and partnership.
- **3** embodies creativity, communication, and sociability. Individuals with a Destiny Number 3 often find success in artistic or communicative roles.
- **4** is associated with stability, organization, and practicality. This number is linked to those who build solid foundations and excel in structured environments.
- **5** represents freedom, adventure, and adaptability. Those with a Destiny Number 5 are often drawn to dynamic roles that offer variety and change.
- **6** stands for responsibility, care, and nurturing. Individuals with this number are often found in roles where they care for others or maintain harmony.
- **7** is linked to introspection, spirituality, and analytical thinking. This number suits those who seek deeper truths and engage in intellectual pursuits.
- **8** represents ambition, power, and material success. People with a Destiny Number 8 are often driven to achieve in business or finance.
- **9** signifies compassion, humanitarianism, and idealism. Individuals with this number are drawn to causes that benefit the greater good.

Master Numbers (11, 22, and 33) hold special significance, representing higher levels of spiritual awareness and potential. For example, a Destiny Number 11 indicates someone who may have a heightened sense of intuition and a calling to inspire others. A Destiny Number 22 is often associated with the ability to turn grand visions into reality, excelling in large-scale projects or leadership roles. Meanwhile, a Destiny Number 33 is linked to selfless service and the role of a teacher or healer, often indicating a life path dedicated to helping others.

The significance of your Destiny Number lies in its ability to illuminate your life's potential. By understanding the traits associated with your number, you can make choices that align with your natural abilities and strengths. For instance, if your Destiny Number is 4, you might thrive in environments that value order and discipline, such as project management or engineering. On the other hand, if your Destiny Number is 5, you might seek out roles that allow for travel, variety, and freedom, such as marketing or sales.

Ultimately, your Destiny Number serves as a roadmap, guiding you toward fulfilling your life's mission. It helps you understand the qualities you were born with and how you can best use them to achieve success and satisfaction. Whether you are naturally creative, analytical, nurturing, or ambitious, your Destiny Number offers insights into how to navigate your life path with purpose and clarity.

How Expression and Destiny Numbers Influence Your Life

The Expression and Destiny Numbers in numerology are concepts for understanding how your inherent traits and potential influence your life's journey. While these numbers are often used interchangeably, they both play distinct roles in shaping your personal and professional experiences. Understanding how these numbers interact and manifest in your life can help you navigate challenges, seize opportunities, and align more closely with your true self.

The Expression Number, calculated from the full name given at birth, reveals the talents and abilities you bring into this world. It reflects the potential you have to fulfill your life's mission, highlighting the qualities that come naturally to you. For example, if your Expression Number is 7, you are likely to be introspective, analytical, and drawn to spiritual or intellectual pursuits. This might lead you to careers or hobbies that involve research, teaching, or exploring the mysteries of life.

The Destiny Number is also derived from your full birth name and is often considered synonymous with the Expression Number. It represents the path you are meant to follow and the goals you are destined to achieve. The Destiny Number is about realizing your potential and using your innate abilities to fulfill your life's purpose. For example, if you have a Destiny Number 8, you might be driven by a strong desire to succeed in business, finance, or any field that involves leadership and management.

These numbers influence your life in several ways. First, they guide you in choosing a career or life path that aligns with your natural talents. For instance, someone with an Expression Number 3, which is associated with creativity and communication, might excel in roles that involve writing, public speaking, or the arts. On the other hand, a person with a Destiny Number 4, linked to organization and discipline, might find fulfillment in careers that require careful planning and execution, such as project management or engineering.

Expression and Destiny Numbers also shape how you approach challenges and opportunities. If your numbers align with the qualities needed to overcome an obstacle, you are more likely to succeed. For example, a person with a Destiny Number 5, which emphasizes adaptability and freedom, might thrive in a dynamic, ever-changing environment where flexibility is key. This person might approach challenges with a sense of adventure, seeing them as opportunities for growth rather than setbacks.

These numbers also play a role in your relationships. Understanding your own Expression and Destiny Numbers can help you better understand your interactions with others. For example, if your Expression Number is 2, you might naturally seek harmony and cooperation in your relationships, often taking on the role of a mediator or peacemaker. Knowing this about yourself can help you navigate conflicts more effectively and build stronger, more supportive relationships.

Moreover, recognizing the Expression and Destiny Numbers of those around you can foster greater empathy and understanding. For instance, if you know that a colleague has a Destiny Number 1, which is linked to leadership and independence, you might better appreciate their need for autonomy and their drive to take charge in projects. This understanding can enhance teamwork and collaboration, allowing you to work more effectively with others by playing to their strengths.

Finally, **Expression and Destiny Numbers influence your sense of fulfillment and purpose**. By aligning your actions with the traits associated with these numbers, you can live a life that feels more authentic and satisfying. For instance, if your Destiny Number suggests a life of service and compassion, such as a 9, you might find the greatest fulfillment in roles that allow you to make a positive impact on the lives of others, whether through social work, teaching, or volunteering.

In essence, Expression and Destiny Numbers provide a blueprint for understanding who you are and what you are meant to do in this life. They guide your decisions, shape your interactions, and help you align with your true purpose. By embracing the qualities these numbers highlight, you can navigate life's journey with greater confidence, clarity, and fulfillment.

Compatibility of Expression Numbers with Other Core Numbers

In numerology, the compatibility of your Expression Number with other core numbers, such as your Life Path, Soul Urge, and Personality Numbers, can provide deep insights into how you navigate life and interact with others. Understanding how these numbers align or conflict can help you achieve balance and harmony in various aspects of your life.

Your **Expression Number** represents your innate talents, abilities, and the path you are meant to follow. It is derived from the full name given at birth and reflects your potential and the qualities you bring into every situation. When this number is in harmony with your other core numbers, you are likely to feel more aligned with your purpose and experience greater ease in achieving your goals.

Expression Number and Life Path Number Compatibility is crucial because your Life Path Number reveals your overall direction in life, while your Expression Number shows how you are likely to achieve that direction. For example, if your Life Path Number is 4, which emphasizes stability, organization, and practicality, and your Expression Number is 8, which is linked to power, ambition, and material success, the compatibility is strong. Both numbers are focused on achievement, though the Life Path Number 4 might emphasize building a solid foundation, while the Expression Number 8 drives towards leadership and accomplishment. This alignment can result in a well-rounded approach to achieving long-term goals.

However, if there is a mismatch between these numbers, challenges can arise. For instance, a Life Path Number 5, which values freedom and adventure, might clash with an Expression Number 4, which seeks order and routine. In this case, the individual might struggle to reconcile their need for flexibility with the drive to create structure. Understanding this conflict allows for a more conscious effort to find balance, perhaps by seeking opportunities that allow for both exploration and organization.

Expression Number and Soul Urge Number Compatibility speaks to the alignment between your outward expressions and your inner desires. The Soul Urge Number, derived from the vowels in your name, reveals your deepest motivations and what you need to feel fulfilled. If your Expression Number is 3, which is associated with creativity and communication, and your Soul Urge Number is 6, which values care, responsibility, and nurturing, there could be a beautiful synergy in pursuing a career in teaching, counseling, or the arts, where both creativity and compassion are essential.

On the other hand, a Soul Urge Number 7, which values introspection and solitude, might feel at odds with an Expression Number 5, which craves change and excitement. This conflict could lead to an inner tension between the desire for quiet reflection and the urge to experience new adventures. Recognizing this dynamic can help you create a lifestyle that honors both needs, perhaps by balancing periods of introspection with times of exploration.

Expression Number and Personality Number Compatibility reveals how your outward persona aligns with your inherent abilities. The Personality Number, derived from the consonants in your name, shows how others perceive you. If your

Expression Number 9, which is linked to humanitarianism and idealism, is paired with a Personality Number 2, which is associated with diplomacy and sensitivity, you might be seen as a compassionate leader who is skilled at bringing people together for a greater cause. This compatibility can enhance your ability to inspire and unite others in both personal and professional settings.

Conversely, a mismatch, such as an Expression Number 8 (ambitious and authoritative) with a Personality Number 3 (lighthearted and expressive), might lead to confusion in how others perceive your intentions. While you might be driven by power and success, others could see you as more playful or less serious. Awareness of this potential disconnect can guide you in managing your image and ensuring that your actions are aligned with how you wish to be perceived.

Understanding the compatibility between your Expression Number and other core numbers offers insights into the dynamics of your personality and life path. By recognizing areas of harmony or conflict, you can make informed choices that align with your true self and navigate life's challenges with greater clarity.

Expression Numbers in Personal and Professional Relationships

Your Expression Number is important in shaping how you interact with others in both personal and professional relationships. This number, which reflects your inherent talents and abilities, influences how you communicate, collaborate, and connect with people around you. Understanding your own Expression Number, as well as those of others, can enhance your relationships by highlighting areas of compatibility and potential conflict.

In personal relationships, your **Expression Number** can reveal how you express love, handle conflict, and support your partner. For example, if you have an Expression Number 2, you are likely to be diplomatic, cooperative, and sensitive to others' needs. In a romantic relationship, this means you might naturally take on the role of peacemaker, striving to create harmony and understanding. You might be particularly attuned to your partner's feelings, making you a supportive and empathetic partner. However, your desire to avoid conflict might also lead to challenges if you tend to suppress your own needs to maintain peace.

If your partner's Expression Number is 5, which is associated with freedom, adventure, and change, the dynamic could be both exciting and challenging. While your partner might bring spontaneity and a sense of adventure to the relationship, their desire for independence might clash with your need for stability and cooperation. Understanding these differences allows you to find ways to balance your partner's need for freedom with your desire for connection, perhaps by supporting each other's individual interests while also nurturing the relationship.

In professional relationships, your Expression Number can influence how you collaborate with colleagues, manage teams, and approach your work. For instance, an **Expression Number 8** is often linked to leadership, ambition, and authority. If you have this number, you might naturally take charge in work situations, driving projects forward with a strong sense of purpose and determination. You are likely to excel in roles that involve decision-making, strategy, and management. However, your authoritative style might sometimes be perceived as domineering, particularly if you work with colleagues who have more sensitive or cooperative Expression Numbers, such as 2 or 6.

In contrast, an **Expression Number 3**, associated with creativity, communication, and sociability, might thrive in environments that encourage brainstorming, collaboration, and innovation. You might be the one who brings fresh ideas to the table and helps to foster a positive and dynamic team atmosphere. However, if you work with someone whose Expression Number is 4, which values structure, discipline, and order, there might be a need to bridge the gap between creativity and practicality. Recognizing this difference can help you find common ground, perhaps by working together to develop creative ideas that are also feasible and well-organized.

Understanding the Expression Numbers of your colleagues or business partners can also guide you in building effective working relationships. For example, if you know that a colleague has an Expression Number 7, which is linked to introspection and analytical thinking, you might approach them for tasks that require deep research or thoughtful analysis. On the other hand, if a team member has an Expression Number 9, associated with humanitarianism and idealism, they might be the ideal person to lead projects that involve social impact or community engagement.

In leadership roles, knowing the Expression Numbers of your team can help you assign tasks that align with each person's strengths, leading to a more harmonious and productive work environment. For example, pairing an Expression Number 1 (leadership and initiative) with an Expression Number 4 (organization and detail-oriented) can create a powerful team dynamic where one person drives the vision while the other ensures that all the details are meticulously managed.

In both personal and professional relationships, understanding Expression Numbers allows you to navigate interactions with greater empathy and effectiveness. By recognizing the unique qualities that each person brings to the table, you can build stronger connections, resolve conflicts more effectively, and create environments where everyone's strengths are valued and utilized.

CHAPTER 4: SOUL URGE NUMBERS

What is a Soul Urge Number?

A Soul Urge Number, sometimes called the Heart's Desire Number, is a central concept in numerology that reveals your deepest desires, motivations, and the driving forces behind your actions. It represents what you truly value and what you seek in life at a core, often subconscious level. While other numerology numbers, like the Life Path or Expression Number, focus on your external traits and life direction, the Soul Urge Number goes into the inner workings of your heart, providing insights into what brings you true fulfillment.

To calculate your Soul Urge Number, you focus on the vowels in your full birth name. Each vowel is assigned a numerical value, following a system where A=1, E=5, I=9, O=6, and U=3. The Y is sometimes considered a vowel depending on its usage in the name. After assigning these values, you sum them and reduce the total to a single digit, unless it's a Master Number like 11 or 22, which isn't reduced further.

Let's go through an example. Suppose your full name is "Emily Rose Taylor." To find your Soul Urge Number, you'd look at the vowels:

- Emily: E = 5, I = 9, and Y (used as a vowel here) = 7. Adding these gives 5 + 9 + 7 = 21, and 2 + 1 = 3.
- Rose: O = 6 and E = 5. Adding these gives 6 + 5 = 11, which is a Master Number and remains 11.
- Taylor: A = 1 and O = 6. Adding these gives 1 + 6 = 7.

Now, sum the results from each part of the name: 3 (from Emily) + 11 (from Rose) + 7 (from Taylor) = 21. Finally, reduce 21 to 2 + 1 = 3. Thus, the Soul Urge Number for Emily Rose Taylor is 3.

The significance of the Soul Urge Number lies in what it reveals about your inner self. For example, a Soul Urge Number 3 indicates a deep desire for creative expression, joy, and social connection. If this is your number, you likely thrive in environments where you can express your ideas, entertain others, and engage in artistic or communicative pursuits. You might find great satisfaction in careers or activities that allow you to be creative and connect with others on an emotional level.

Each Soul Urge Number from 1 to 9, along with the Master Numbers 11 and 22, carries its own unique set of meanings:

- **1** reflects a desire for independence, leadership, and personal achievement. You likely value autonomy and are driven to make your mark on the world.
- **2** indicates a deep need for harmony, partnership, and cooperation. You may find fulfillment in nurturing relationships and working closely with others.
- **3** embodies a love for creativity, communication, and joy. You are drawn to artistic expression and seek to spread positivity.
- **4** represents a desire for stability, order, and practicality. You might value structure and enjoy building a secure, organized life.
- **5** suggests a craving for freedom, adventure, and variety. You likely seek new experiences and are always looking for ways to break free from routine.
- **6** reflects a need for love, care, and responsibility. You are often drawn to roles where you can support and nurture others.
- **7** indicates a desire for introspection, spiritual growth, and deep knowledge. You likely value solitude and are drawn to exploring life's mysteries.
- **8** suggests a strong drive for power, success, and material abundance. You are motivated to achieve and leave a lasting impact on the world.
- **9** reflects a deep compassion, idealism, and a desire to serve humanity. You are likely drawn to causes that benefit the greater good.
- **11** is a Master Number indicating a heightened intuition, spiritual insight, and a mission to inspire others. You may feel a strong inner calling to lead and uplift those around you.
- **22** is also a Master Number, representing the potential to turn grand visions into reality. You likely have a powerful drive to build something meaningful and lasting.

Understanding your Soul Urge Number provides valuable insight into your true motivations and what you need to feel fulfilled. For example, if your Soul Urge Number is 6, you might find that you are most content when caring for others, creating a harmonious home environment, or working in a profession that allows you to support and nurture. Recognizing this about yourself can guide you in making life choices that align with your inner desires, leading to a more satisfying and authentic life.

Your Soul Urge Number acts as a compass, pointing you toward what truly resonates with your heart. By aligning your actions and decisions with the qualities revealed by this number, you can live a life that is more in tune with your deepest aspirations and emotional needs. Whether in your relationships, career, or personal pursuits, understanding your Soul Urge Number helps you focus on what will bring you the greatest joy and fulfillment.

Discovering Your Soul Urge Number

Discovering your Soul Urge Number is a revealing process that taps into the core of your emotional and spiritual motivations. This number, also known as the Heart's Desire Number, uncovers what truly drives you, providing insight into your inner self. Calculating your Soul Urge Number involves analyzing the vowels in your full birth name, as these letters are believed to resonate with your soul's deepest needs.

To calculate your Soul Urge Number, assign numerical values to the vowels in your name using the following system: A=1, E=5, I=9, O=6, U=3. The letter Y is sometimes counted as a vowel if it acts like one in your name. After assigning these values, add them together and reduce the total to a single digit, unless it results in a Master Number (11 or 22), which is not reduced further.

Let's work through an example. Imagine your full name is "Michael Andrew Smith." To find your Soul Urge Number, you would examine the vowels in each part of the name:

- Michael: I = 9, A = 1, E = 5. Adding these together gives 9 + 1 + 5 = 15, and then 1 + 5 = 6.
- Andrew: A = 1, E = 5. Adding these gives 1 + 5 = 6.
- Smith: I = 9. Since there's only one vowel, the sum is 9.

Now, add the results from each part of the name: 6 (from Michael) + 6 (from Andrew) + 9 (from Smith) = 21. Finally, reduce 21 by adding 2 + 1, which equals 3. Therefore, the Soul Urge Number for Michael Andrew Smith is 3.

Another example might involve a name like "Olivia Grace Johnson." The vowels are:

- Olivia: O = 6, I = 9, I = 9, A = 1. The sum is 6 + 9 + 9 + 1 = 25, and 2 + 5 = 7.
- Grace: A = 1, E = 5. The sum is 1 + 5 = 6.
- Johnson: O = 6. The sum is 6.

Adding these together gives 7 (from Olivia) + 6 (from Grace) + 6 (from Johnson) = 19. Reducing 19 gives 1 + 9 = 10, and then 1 + 0 = 1. Olivia Grace Johnson has a Soul Urge Number of 1.

Your Soul Urge Number offers insights into your most profound desires, guiding you toward what truly fulfills you. Whether your number indicates a deep need for creativity, love, stability, or freedom, discovering it can help you better understand yourself and make choices that align with your heart's true yearnings.

How Soul Urge Influences Your Desires and Motivations

Your Soul Urge Number is a key driver of your desires, shaping the way you approach life and influencing the choices you make. It reflects your innermost needs and what you truly seek in life, often guiding your decisions even when you're not consciously aware of it. Understanding this number can help you recognize why certain things are important to you and why you're motivated to pursue specific goals.

For instance, if your Soul Urge Number is 2, you are likely driven by a deep need for harmony, partnership, and emotional connection. This might manifest in your strong desire to build close relationships, whether in your personal life or at work. You might find that you are most content when you are part of a team or in a partnership where mutual support and understanding are key. This desire for connection can influence your career choices, leading you toward roles in counseling, mediation, or any field where collaboration is essential.

On the other hand, if your Soul Urge Number is 5, your core desire might revolve around freedom, adventure, and variety. You are likely motivated by the need to experience new things, explore different environments, and break free from routines. This urge might lead you to seek out travel opportunities, change careers frequently, or take on projects that offer a high degree of flexibility. You might feel restless in situations that are too predictable or confined, always looking for the next adventure or challenge that keeps life exciting.

A Soul Urge Number 7 suggests a strong desire for knowledge, introspection, and spiritual growth. If this is your number, you are likely motivated by a quest for understanding the deeper meanings of life. You might be drawn to study, research, or spiritual practices that allow you to explore these questions. This influence could guide you toward careers in academia, science, or spirituality, where your need for depth and introspection can be fulfilled.

Meanwhile, a Soul Urge Number 8 is driven by a desire for power, success, and material achievement. If this is your number, you might be motivated by the ambition to achieve great things and leave a lasting legacy. You likely thrive in environments where you can take charge, make decisions, and drive progress. This desire for success might lead you toward leadership roles in business, finance, or politics, where you can exert influence and achieve tangible results.

Aligning Your Life with Your Soul Urge

Aligning your life with your Soul Urge Number is about making choices that resonate with your deepest desires and inner motivations. When your actions and decisions are in harmony with your Soul Urge, you are more likely to experience fulfillment and a sense of purpose. This alignment helps you live authentically, in a way that truly satisfies your heart's desires.

For example, if your Soul Urge Number is 6, you are naturally inclined toward care, responsibility, and nurturing. You might find that you are happiest when you are taking care of others, whether in your family, community, or profession. Aligning your life with this number might involve pursuing a career in healthcare, education, or social work, where you can use your nurturing abilities to help others. In your personal life, you might focus on creating a loving, supportive home environment or volunteering for causes that involve caring for those in need.

If your Soul Urge Number is 9, you are driven by compassion, humanitarianism, and a desire to serve the greater good. To align with this number, you might choose to engage in activities that allow you to make a positive impact on the world. This could involve working for a non-profit organization, advocating for social justice, or dedicating time to charitable causes. In your personal life, you might focus on fostering connections with others and finding ways to contribute to your community. This alignment not only fulfills your need to serve but also enhances your sense of purpose and meaning in life.

A Soul Urge Number 1 reflects a desire for independence, leadership, and personal achievement. If this is your number, aligning with it might mean pursuing goals that allow you to assert your individuality and take charge of your destiny. You might find fulfillment in entrepreneurship, where you can build something of your own, or in leadership roles where you can guide others and make decisions that shape the future. In your personal life, you might seek out opportunities that allow you to be self-sufficient and express your unique vision.

For those with a Soul Urge Number 4, the desire for stability, order, and practicality is paramount. Aligning your life with this number might involve focusing on creating a structured, organized environment where you can thrive. You might be drawn to careers in project management, engineering, or accounting, where attention to detail and a methodical approach are valued. In your personal life, you might prioritize building a secure foundation, such as owning a home or saving for the future, which provides you with the stability you crave.

Aligning your life with your Soul Urge Number isn't about rigidly following a path, but rather about making choices that feel right to your innermost self. By understanding and embracing your Soul Urge, you can make decisions that lead to a more fulfilling and authentic life, where your actions are in harmony with your deepest desires and motivations. This alignment not only brings satisfaction but also helps you live with greater intention and purpose, fully embracing who you are at your core.

CHAPTER 5: PERSONALITY NUMBERS

Understanding Personality Numbers

A Personality Number in numerology reveals how others perceive you, offering insight into the outer layer of your personality. It's the first impression you give, the traits that are most visible to others. While your Life Path Number or Soul Urge Number might reflect your deeper desires and life purpose, the Personality Number is about how you present yourself to the world and how people respond to that presentation.

To calculate your Personality Number, you focus on the consonants in your full birth name. Each consonant is assigned a numerical value based on its position in the alphabet (A=1, B=2, C=3, and so on). You then sum these values and reduce the total to a single digit, unless it results in a Master Number like 11 or 22, which is not reduced further.

For example, let's take the name "Sophia Grace Smith." To find the Personality Number, look at the consonants:

- Sophia: S = 1, P = 7, H = 8, and the sum is 1 + 7 + 8 = 16, then 1 + 6 = 7.
- Grace: G = 7, R = 9, C = 3, and the sum is 7 + 9 + 3 = 19, then 1 + 9 = 10, and 1 + 0 = 1.
- Smith: S = 1, M = 4, T = 2, H = 8, and the sum is 1 + 4 + 2 + 8 = 15, then 1 + 5 = 6.

Now, add the results: 7 (from Sophia) + 1 (from Grace) + 6 (from Smith) = 14, and 1 + 4 = 5. Therefore, Sophia Grace Smith's Personality Number is 5.

Personality Numbers range from 1 to 9, each with distinct characteristics:

- **1** indicates a strong, independent personality. You are seen as a leader, someone who is confident and capable. People might view you as assertive and ambitious, often taking the initiative in situations.
- **2** reflects a more sensitive and cooperative nature. You are perceived as diplomatic, understanding, and willing to work with others. People might come to you for advice or mediation because of your calm and balanced approach.
- **3** suggests a lively, creative, and expressive personality. Others see you as fun, outgoing, and full of ideas. You likely make a strong impression in social settings, where your communication skills shine.

- **4** represents a practical, reliable, and grounded personality. You are seen as someone who is dependable and organized. People might view you as a hard worker who values stability and order.
- **5** indicates a dynamic, adventurous, and adaptable personality. You are perceived as someone who loves change and thrives on variety. Others might see you as energetic, open-minded, and always on the move.
- **6** reflects a nurturing, responsible, and caring personality. You are seen as someone who is supportive and protective. People might view you as a caretaker, often putting the needs of others before your own.
- **7** suggests a thoughtful, introspective, and sometimes mysterious personality. Others might see you as reserved, intellectual, and deeply reflective. You are likely perceived as someone who values privacy and deep thinking.
- **8** represents a strong, ambitious, and authoritative personality. You are seen as someone who is driven to succeed and often takes on leadership roles. People might view you as powerful and focused on achieving your goals.
- **9** indicates a compassionate, generous, and humanitarian personality. You are perceived as someone who cares deeply about others and is often involved in helping or supporting causes. People might see you as idealistic and committed to making the world a better place.

Master Numbers 11 and 22 bring additional layers of complexity. If your Personality Number is 11, you might be seen as someone with a strong intuition and spiritual presence, often inspiring others. A Personality Number 22 might make you appear as a master builder, someone who is capable of creating significant and lasting impacts in the world.

Understanding your Personality Number helps you recognize how you come across to others. This awareness can be valuable in both personal and professional settings. For example, if you have a Personality Number 7, you might be seen as reserved or aloof, which could affect how others approach you. Knowing this, you can choose to be more open in situations where you want to build closer relationships.

On the other hand, if your Personality Number is 3, you might naturally draw people in with your charisma and creativity, making you well-suited for roles that involve public speaking or social interaction. Being aware of how you are perceived allows you to leverage your strengths and address any potential misunderstandings.

In essence, your Personality Number offers a glimpse into how others see you, providing insights that can help you navigate social dynamics with greater confidence and clarity. Whether you're aiming to enhance your personal connections or improve your professional image, understanding your Personality Number is a valuable step in aligning how you are perceived with who you truly are.

Calculating Your Personality Number

Calculating your Personality Number in numerology involves focusing on the consonants in your full birth name. This number reveals how others perceive you, providing insights into the traits and qualities that are most visible to those around you. It's an essential aspect of numerology that helps you understand the first impressions you create.

To calculate your Personality Number, you'll need to assign numerical values to each consonant in your full birth name. Numerology uses a system where A=1, B=2, C=3, and so on, with the following values for consonants:

- B = 2, C = 3, D = 4, F = 6, G = 7, H = 8, J = 1, K = 2, L = 3, M = 4, N = 5, P = 7, Q = 8, R = 9, S = 1, T = 2, V = 4, W = 5, X = 6, Y = 7, Z = 8.

Let's walk through an example using the name "James Arthur Wilson." To calculate the Personality Number, focus on the consonants:

- James: J = 1, M = 4, S = 1. Adding these together gives 1 + 4 + 1 = 6.
- Arthur: R = 9, T = 2, H = 8, R = 9. Adding these together gives 9 + 2 + 8 + 9 = 28, and 2 + 8 = 10, then 1 + 0 = 1.
- Wilson: W = 5, L = 3, S = 1, N = 5. Adding these together gives 5 + 3 + 1 + 5 = 14, and 1 + 4 = 5.

Now, sum the results from each part of the name: 6 (from James) + 1 (from Arthur) + 5 (from Wilson) = 12, and 1 + 2 = 3. Therefore, James Arthur Wilson's Personality Number is 3.

Another example is the name "Elizabeth Grace Scott." The consonants are:

- Elizabeth: L = 3, Z = 8, B = 2, T = 2, H = 8. The sum is 3 + 8 + 2 + 2 + 8 = 23, and 2 + 3 = 5.
- Grace: G = 7, R = 9, C = 3. The sum is 7 + 9 + 3 = 19, and 1 + 9 = 10, then 1 + 0 = 1.
- Scott: S = 1, C = 3, T = 2, T = 2. The sum is 1 + 3 + 2 + 2 = 8.

Adding these together gives 5 (from Elizabeth) + 1 (from Grace) + 8 (from Scott) = 14, and 1 + 4 = 5. Elizabeth Grace Scott's Personality Number is 5.

Your Personality Number helps you understand how you come across to others, influencing their initial impressions and interactions with you. By recognizing this number, you can gain insights into the traits you naturally project, helping you navigate social situations more effectively and align your outer persona with your true self.

How Personality Numbers Shape First Impressions

Personality Numbers in numerology are important in shaping the first impressions you make on others. This number reflects the outer layer of your personality—the traits and qualities that are most apparent to those you meet. Understanding your Personality Number can help you manage how others perceive you, allowing you to create the impression you want to make.

For example, if your Personality Number is 1, you are likely perceived as confident, assertive, and independent. You may come across as a natural leader, someone who takes charge in situations and isn't afraid to stand out. This can be advantageous in professional settings where leadership qualities are valued, but it might also lead others to see you as overly dominant or unapproachable if not balanced with warmth and openness.

A Personality Number 2, on the other hand, suggests that you are seen as diplomatic, cooperative, and empathetic. You likely make an impression as someone who is easy to talk to and who values harmony in relationships. This can make you well-liked and trusted in both personal and professional settings, particularly in roles that require collaboration and mediation. However, others might also perceive you as overly passive or hesitant to take a stand if they don't recognize your strength in diplomacy.

If your Personality Number is 3, you are likely perceived as outgoing, creative, and expressive. People might see you as charismatic and entertaining, someone who brings energy and positivity to social situations. This can make you a magnet in social circles and valuable in roles that require communication and creativity. However, if not balanced, others might also see you as superficial or overly focused on being the center of attention.

For those with a Personality Number 7, the impression you give might be one of depth, introspection, and mystery. You might come across as someone who is thoughtful and reserved, often seen as a thinker or intellectual. This can be appealing to those who value deep conversations and intellectual pursuits, but it might also make you seem distant or aloof to others who prefer more straightforward social interactions.

Understanding how your Personality Number shapes first impressions allows you to be more mindful of how you present yourself. For instance, if you have a Personality Number 8, which is associated with power, ambition, and authority, you might naturally command respect and attention in professional settings. However, if you're aware that this might also make you seem intimidating, you can consciously balance this with a more approachable demeanor when needed.

By recognizing the influence of your Personality Number, you can manage the way others perceive you, ensuring that the first impression you make aligns with your intentions and the image you wish to project. This awareness can enhance your social interactions, helping you build stronger connections and navigate different social environments with confidence.

Balancing Personality with Other Core Numbers

In numerology, balancing your Personality Number with your other core numbers, such as your Life Path, Soul Urge, and Expression Numbers, is essential for achieving harmony in how you present yourself and live your life. Each of these numbers reflects different aspects of your identity, and understanding how they interact can help you align your outer persona with your true self.

For example, if your **Personality Number is 4**, you are likely perceived as reliable, practical, and grounded. However, if your Life Path Number is 5, which is associated with adventure, freedom, and change, there might be an internal conflict between your desire for stability (reflected in your Personality Number) and your need for variety and new experiences (reflected in your Life Path Number). Balancing these numbers might involve finding ways to incorporate both stability and adventure into your life, such as pursuing a stable career while seeking adventure through travel or hobbies.

If you have a **Personality Number 6**, you might be seen as nurturing, responsible, and caring. However, if your Soul Urge Number is 7, which values introspection, solitude, and intellectual pursuits, you might struggle to balance your outward nurturing persona with your inner need for solitude and reflection. In this case, you might find it beneficial to carve out time for yourself, ensuring that your need for quiet and introspection is met while still fulfilling your role as a caregiver.

For those with a **Personality Number 8**, you might project an image of power, ambition, and authority. If your Expression Number is 2, which emphasizes diplomacy, cooperation, and sensitivity, you might find a need to balance your assertive personality with a more gentle and cooperative approach. This balance can be crucial in leadership roles, where you need to assert authority while also working effectively with others and maintaining harmonious relationships.

Another example is a **Personality Number 3**, which is outgoing, creative, and expressive. If paired with a Life Path Number 9, which is associated with compassion, humanitarianism, and a desire to serve others, you might find that balancing your need for personal expression with a commitment to helping others is key to feeling fulfilled. This might involve channeling your creativity into causes that benefit the greater good, such as using your talents in art or communication to raise awareness for social issues.

Understanding how to balance your Personality Number with other core numbers allows you to live more authentically and align your actions with your true self. It helps you integrate the various aspects of your personality, ensuring that your outer presentation is consistent with your inner values and desires. This balance not only enhances your personal and professional relationships but also contributes to a greater sense of harmony and fulfillment in your life.

By recognizing the interplay between your Personality Number and other core numbers, you can make more informed decisions that reflect your whole self, leading to a more balanced and satisfying life. Whether it's finding the right career path, building strong relationships, or pursuing personal growth, achieving this balance is key to living a life that truly resonates with who you are.

CHAPTER 6: BIRTH DAY NUMBERS

The Importance of Your Birth Day Number

Your Birth Day Number in numerology is a key piece of your personal profile, representing the specific day of the month you were born. This number offers unique insights into your innate talents, characteristics, and potential challenges. Unlike your Life Path Number, which provides a broad overview of your life's journey, the Birth Day Number zeroes in on the specific traits that are naturally yours, often highlighting the special qualities you possess from birth.

Each day of the month carries its own vibration, and this vibration influences your personality in a way that is distinct and immediately impactful. For example, if you were born on the 1st of any month, your Birth Day Number is 1. This number is associated with leadership, independence, and a pioneering spirit. People born on the 1st tend to be self-starters, often drawn to roles where they can take the lead and innovate. They are naturally confident and have a strong drive to achieve their goals.

Being born on the 15th, however, gives you a different energy. The Birth Day Number 15 is a combination of the energies of 1 and 5, reduced to 6. This suggests a blend of independence and adaptability (from 1 and 5) with a nurturing and responsible nature (from the 6). People with this Birth Day Number are often drawn to careers or roles where they can care for others while also maintaining a sense of personal freedom. They might excel in fields like healthcare, education, or any area that involves service and community.

If you were born on the 22nd, your Birth Day Number is one of the Master Numbers, which adds another layer of significance. The number 22 is often referred to as the "Master Builder," representing the ability to turn dreams into reality through hard work, discipline, and a visionary approach. People born on the 22nd might feel a strong sense of purpose, often driven to create something lasting and meaningful. This number suggests a natural ability to take on large-scale projects or leadership roles that require both practicality and a visionary mindset.

Your Birth Day Number is not just a number—it's a reflection of the specific strengths and tendencies that you bring into every situation. For example, someone born on the 11th has a Birth Day Number 11, another Master Number. This number is often associated with intuition, spiritual insight, and the ability to inspire others. People with this Birth Day Number might find that they have a natural ability to understand things on a deeper level, often being drawn to roles that involve teaching, counseling, or any field where they can share their unique insights.

On the other hand, a Birth Day Number 4, which comes from being born on the 4th, 13th, 22nd, or 31st, is associated with practicality, organization, and a methodical approach to life. People with this Birth Day Number are often seen as reliable, hard-working, and detail-oriented. They are likely to excel in roles that require precision and attention to detail, such as engineering, accounting, or project management.

The importance of your Birth Day Number lies in how it can help you understand the natural talents and characteristics that you might take for granted. For instance, if you were born on the 7th, your Birth Day Number is 7, which is associated with introspection, spirituality, and analytical thinking. You might naturally be drawn to study, research, or spiritual exploration, finding satisfaction in activities that allow you to go into the mysteries of life.

Understanding your Birth Day Number helps you recognize the unique gifts you bring to the world. It offers a clearer picture of why certain things come easily to you and why you might gravitate toward specific activities or career paths. By embracing the qualities highlighted by your Birth Day Number, you can make more informed choices that align with your natural strengths, leading to a more fulfilling and authentic life.

How to Calculate Your Birth Day Number

Calculating your Birth Day Number in numerology is a straightforward process that focuses on the exact day of the month you were born. This number is significant because it represents specific talents, tendencies, and traits that are naturally yours. It's one of the simplest calculations in numerology, yet it offers profound insights into your character.

To calculate your Birth Day Number, you simply use the day of the month on which you were born. This number doesn't need to be reduced unless it's a double-digit number between 10 and 31. If your birth date is a single digit (1-9), that number is your Birth Day Number. If it's a double digit, you add the two digits together to get a single digit, unless the result is 11, 22, or 33, which are considered Master Numbers.

For example, if you were born on the 7th of any month, your Birth Day Number is 7. This number is associated with introspection, spirituality, and analytical thinking. If you were born on the 18th, you would add 1 + 8, resulting in 9, which is your Birth Day Number. The number 9 is often linked to compassion, humanitarianism, and a strong sense of idealism.

Let's consider another example: a person born on the 22nd. In numerology, 22 is a Master Number, so it's not reduced further. As a Master Number, 22 is often referred to as the "Master Builder," indicating a person with the potential to turn ambitious dreams into reality through hard work, dedication, and a practical approach. People with this Birth Day Number are believed to have the potential for significant achievements, particularly in areas that involve large-scale projects or leadership roles.

If you were born on the 29th, you would add 2 + 9, which equals 11. Here, 11 is another Master Number, often associated with spiritual insight, intuition, and the ability to inspire others. Individuals with this Birth Day Number might feel a strong calling to engage in work that involves teaching, counseling, or guiding others through their wisdom and understanding.

For those born on the 14th, the calculation involves adding 1 + 4, which equals 5. The number 5 is associated with freedom, adventure, and versatility. People with this Birth Day Number are often seen as dynamic, adaptable, and always ready for change. They may find satisfaction in careers or lifestyles that allow them to explore new experiences and avoid routine.

Even those born on days like the 1st or the 30th can find meaning in their Birth Day Number. For example, being born on the 1st associates you with leadership, independence, and a pioneering spirit. If your birthday is on the 30th, you add 3 + 0, resulting in 3, a number linked to creativity, expression, and sociability.

In summary, calculating your Birth Day Number is as simple as looking at the day you were born and reducing it to a single digit or recognizing it as a Master Number. This number provides a clear snapshot of specific characteristics and talents you naturally possess, offering a valuable tool for self-understanding and personal growth.

The Influence of Birth Day Numbers on Personal Traits

Your Birth Day Number in numerology helps in shaping your personal traits and characteristics. Each number from 1 to 31 carries its own unique energy and influence, affecting how you interact with the world, how you approach challenges, and what innate talents you bring to your life's journey.

For instance, if you have a Birth Day Number of 1, you are likely to exhibit strong leadership qualities. People with this number tend to be independent, self-motivated, and capable of taking charge in various situations. They often possess a pioneering spirit, always looking to innovate and lead rather than follow. This natural inclination towards leadership can make them excel in roles where decision-making and initiative are key.

On the other hand, if your Birth Day Number is 2, your traits are likely to revolve around cooperation, diplomacy, and sensitivity. People born on the 2nd often have a strong ability to work with others, valuing harmony and partnership. They might excel in environments where teamwork is essential, such as in mediation, counseling, or any role that requires understanding and empathy. The gentle and cooperative nature of a Birth Day Number 2 person often makes them well-liked and appreciated in social settings.

A Birth Day Number of 5 brings a different energy, associated with freedom, adventure, and versatility. Individuals with this number tend to thrive in dynamic environments that offer variety and excitement. They are adaptable, curious, and always eager to explore new ideas and experiences. This makes them well-suited for careers or lifestyles that involve travel, change, and constant learning. However, their love for freedom can sometimes make them restless or resistant to routine.

Those with a Birth Day Number of 8 are often seen as ambitious, practical, and focused on success. This number is linked to power, material wealth, and the ability to manage large projects or enterprises. People born on the 8th often have a strong sense of determination and are driven to achieve their goals. They are natural leaders in the business world and may find satisfaction in roles that involve management, finance, or entrepreneurship.

A Birth Day Number of 9, however, is associated with compassion, idealism, and a strong sense of humanitarianism. People with this number are often drawn to helping others and making a positive impact on the world. They are likely to be involved in charitable work, activism, or any field that allows them to express their deep concern for the welfare of others. The idealistic nature of a Birth Day Number 9 person often leads them to pursue causes that benefit the greater good.

Master Numbers like 11 and 22 bring an additional layer of complexity and potential. For example, a Birth Day Number of 11 is associated with spiritual insight, intuition, and the ability to inspire others. People with this number might feel a strong calling to guide or mentor others, often finding themselves in roles that involve teaching, counseling, or leadership in spiritual or creative fields. Similarly, a Birth Day Number of 22, known as the "Master Builder," is associated with the ability to turn dreams into reality. Individuals with this number are often highly ambitious, disciplined, and capable of achieving great things, especially in areas that involve large-scale projects or leadership.

Understanding how your Birth Day Number influences your personal traits can provide insights into your strengths and challenges. It helps you recognize the qualities that are naturally yours and guides you in making decisions that align with your true self. Whether it's pursuing a career, building relationships, or navigating life's challenges, knowing your Birth Day Number offers a clearer understanding of the path that resonates with who you are.

Using Birth Day Numbers to Enhance Life Decisions

Your Birth Day Number in numerology is more than just a reflection of your personality traits—it's a tool that can guide you in making important life decisions. By understanding the unique energies associated with your Birth Day Number, you can align your choices with your natural strengths, preferences, and inclinations, leading to more fulfilling outcomes.

For example, if your Birth Day Number is 3, which is associated with creativity, communication, and social interaction, you might find that decisions involving artistic expression or public speaking are particularly beneficial for you. When faced with career choices, you might thrive in environments that allow you to use your creative talents, such as in writing, design, or marketing. Knowing this can help you steer away from roles that are overly analytical or isolating, which might not resonate with your natural inclinations.

On the other hand, if you have a Birth Day Number of 7, which is linked to introspection, spirituality, and analytical thinking, you might be better suited to decisions that involve deep thinking, research, or solitary work. When choosing a career path, you might excel in fields like academia, scientific research, or spiritual counseling. This understanding can guide you away from high-energy, extroverted roles that might feel overwhelming or draining for you.

For those with a Birth Day Number of 8, which is associated with ambition, authority, and material success, decisions related to business, finance, or leadership are likely to be rewarding. You might find that you are naturally drawn to roles that involve management, entrepreneurship, or financial planning. Knowing your Birth Day Number can help you pursue opportunities that align with your drive for success and avoid situations that don't offer the potential for growth and advancement.

If your Birth Day Number is 2, associated with cooperation, diplomacy, and partnership, you might find that decisions involving teamwork or relationship-building are where you excel. When making life choices, whether in your career or personal life, you might prioritize environments where collaboration is key. This can also help you recognize the importance of finding balance and harmony in your relationships, guiding you in making decisions that foster mutual respect and understanding.

A Birth Day Number of 5, linked to freedom, adventure, and adaptability, suggests that you thrive in situations that offer variety and change. When making decisions, whether it's choosing a job, a place to live, or even planning your day-to-day activities, you might seek out opportunities that allow for exploration and flexibility. This understanding can help you avoid committing to situations that feel too restrictive or monotonous, ensuring that your choices support your need for independence and excitement.

For those with a Birth Day Number of 9, which is associated with compassion, humanitarianism, and idealism, decisions that involve helping others or working for a cause might be especially fulfilling. You might be drawn to careers in social work, activism, or any field that allows you to contribute to the greater good. Recognizing this can guide you toward decisions that align with your desire to make a positive impact, rather than pursuing paths that are purely self-serving.

By using your Birth Day Number as a guide, you can make decisions that not only resonate with your natural traits but also enhance your overall life satisfaction. Whether it's choosing a career, building relationships, or navigating personal challenges, understanding the influence of your Birth Day Number can help you make choices that are more in tune with who you truly are.

Birth Day Numbers and Life Events

Your Birth Day Number in numerology can also provide insights into how you experience and respond to significant life events. This number influences your natural reactions to challenges and opportunities, shaping the way you navigate pivotal moments in your life.

For instance, if you have a Birth Day Number of 1, which is associated with leadership, independence, and a pioneering spirit, you are likely to approach life events with confidence and determination. Whether it's starting a new job, moving to a different city, or beginning a new relationship, you are naturally inclined to take charge and initiate action. Life events that require you to step up, make decisions, and lead others will likely bring out the best in you. However, this same energy can also lead to impatience or a tendency to dominate situations, so it's important to be mindful of how you balance assertiveness with collaboration.

If your Birth Day Number is 4, linked to stability, organization, and practicality, you are likely to approach life events with a methodical and disciplined mindset. When faced with major changes, such as buying a house, planning a wedding, or managing a career transition, you might find comfort in creating detailed plans and establishing routines. Your natural inclination towards order and structure can help you manage complex situations with ease. However, life events that are chaotic or unpredictable might feel challenging for you, so finding ways to create stability in such moments can be key to your well-being.

A Birth Day Number of 6, associated with responsibility, care, and nurturing, suggests that you might approach life events with a focus on supporting others and maintaining harmony. Whether it's welcoming a new family member, dealing with a loved one's illness, or navigating a personal crisis, your instinct is likely to be one of care and protection. You might find yourself taking on the role of a caregiver, ensuring that everyone around you is supported. This can be incredibly rewarding, but it's also important to ensure that you don't neglect your own needs in the process.

For those with a Birth Day Number of 9, which is linked to compassion, humanitarianism, and idealism, life events are often seen through the lens of a broader purpose. You might be particularly moved by events that involve social justice, community service, or helping others in need. Major life decisions, such as choosing a career or starting a family, might be influenced by your desire to make a positive impact on the world. However, this idealism can sometimes lead to frustration if the realities of life don't align with your vision, so finding ways to channel your energy into meaningful action is crucial.

If you have a Birth Day Number of 5, characterized by freedom, adventure, and adaptability, you are likely to approach life events with a sense of curiosity and excitement. Whether it's traveling to a new country, changing careers, or exploring new hobbies, you thrive on the opportunities that change brings. Life events that involve new experiences and personal growth are likely to be particularly fulfilling for you. However, the desire for freedom can also lead to restlessness, so it's important to balance your need for adventure with the commitments and responsibilities that come with major life events.

Understanding how your Birth Day Number influences your response to life events can help you navigate these moments with greater awareness and intention. By recognizing the traits and tendencies associated with your number, you can approach significant life changes in a way that aligns with your natural strengths, leading to more positive and fulfilling experiences.

CHAPTER 7: PERSONAL YEAR NUMBERS

Introduction to Personal Year Cycles

In numerology, the concept of Personal Year Cycles offers a unique perspective on the unfolding of your life's journey. Each year carries its own vibrational energy, influencing the events, opportunities, and challenges you may encounter. Understanding your Personal Year Number can help you align your actions with the natural flow of these cycles, making the most of each phase in your life.

To calculate your Personal Year Number, you add the digits of your birth day and month to the digits of the current year. For example, if you were born on April 15 and you want to know your Personal Year Number for 2024, you would calculate it as follows: 4 (for April) + 15 (1 + 5 = 6) + 2024 (2 + 0 + 2 + 4 = 8). Adding these together gives 4 + 6 + 8 = 18, and then 1 + 8 = 9. So, your Personal Year Number for 2024 is 9.

Each Personal Year Number from 1 to 9 represents a distinct phase in your life cycle:

- **Personal Year 1** is all about new beginnings. It's a year of fresh starts, where you might feel an urge to embark on new projects or make significant changes in your life. This is a time to focus on your goals, take initiative, and embrace independence. For example, you might find yourself starting a new job, moving to a new place, or beginning a new relationship.
- **Personal Year 2** emphasizes cooperation, relationships, and patience. After the bold actions of a Year 1, this year encourages you to focus on partnerships and building connections. It's a time for nurturing relationships, both personal and professional, and for working collaboratively with others. This might be a year where you need to practice diplomacy and sensitivity in your interactions.
- **Personal Year 3** brings creativity, communication, and social expansion. It's a year to express yourself, whether through artistic endeavors, writing, or speaking. Social interactions are highlighted, and you may find yourself more outgoing and interested in connecting with others. This is a great time to pursue hobbies, share your ideas, and engage with the world in a vibrant way.
- **Personal Year 4** is about building foundations, discipline, and hard work. It's a year to focus on stability and structure, where you might be drawn to organizing your life, setting long-term goals, and working steadily toward them. This could involve managing your finances, improving your health, or committing to a major project that requires persistence and attention to detail.

- **Personal Year 5** introduces change, freedom, and adventure. After the steady progress of a Year 4, this year encourages you to embrace new experiences and be open to unexpected opportunities. It's a time to explore, travel, and break free from routines. You might find yourself making sudden changes, whether in your career, lifestyle, or personal relationships.
- **Personal Year 6** focuses on responsibility, family, and community. It's a year to pay attention to your home life and the well-being of those around you. You might be called upon to take on more responsibility, whether it's caring for a loved one, improving your home environment, or contributing to your community. This year is about balance, harmony, and nurturing relationships.
- **Personal Year 7** is a time for introspection, spiritual growth, and self-discovery. It's a year to step back from the busyness of life and focus on your inner world. You might feel drawn to study, meditate, or explore philosophical and spiritual questions. This is a time for personal growth, where you can gain deep insights into yourself and the direction you want your life to take.
- **Personal Year 8** emphasizes power, success, and achievement. It's a year to focus on your career, financial goals, and personal ambitions. This is a time to step into leadership roles, take charge of your life, and manifest your desires into reality. You might find opportunities for advancement in your career or ways to increase your financial stability.
- **Personal Year 9** marks the end of a cycle, bringing completion, reflection, and letting go. It's a year to tie up loose ends, release what no longer serves you, and prepare for new beginnings in the next cycle. This might involve ending relationships, leaving a job, or simply reflecting on what you've learned over the past years. It's a time for forgiveness, compassion, and making peace with the past.

Understanding your Personal Year Number allows you to navigate each year with greater awareness and intention. By aligning your actions with the natural energy of the year, you can make decisions that support your growth and well-being, whether you're starting something new, building on what you've achieved, or letting go to make space for the future. Each year offers a unique opportunity for personal development, and knowing where you are in your Personal Year Cycle can help you make the most of it.

How to Determine Your Personal Year Number

Determining your Personal Year Number in numerology is a simple process that reveals the energy and themes you'll experience throughout the year. This number helps you understand the influences at play in your life, guiding you to make the most of the opportunities and challenges that arise.

To calculate your Personal Year Number, start with the month and day of your birth, and add them to the current year. Let's break this down with an example.

Suppose your birthday is March 15, and you want to determine your Personal Year Number for 2024. First, you convert your birth month and day into numbers: March is the 3rd month, and 15 is already a number.

- Birth month: 3
- Birth day: 15 (1 + 5 = 6)
- Current year: 2024 (2 + 0 + 2 + 4 = 8)

Now, add these numbers together: 3 (for March) + 6 (from 15) + 8 (from 2024) = 17. Finally, reduce 17 to a single digit by adding 1 + 7, which equals 8. So, your Personal Year Number for 2024 is 8.

Let's consider another example. If someone was born on November 22 and wants to find their Personal Year Number for 2024:

- Birth month: November is the 11th month (1 + 1 = 2)
- Birth day: 22 (since 22 is a Master Number, it stays as is)
- Current year: 2024 (2 + 0 + 2 + 4 = 8)

Add these together: 2 (for November) + 22 (Master Number) + 8 (from 2024) = 32. Reduce 32 by adding 3 + 2, which equals 5. Therefore, the Personal Year Number for this person in 2024 is 5.

Understanding your Personal Year Number can offer you insights into the themes that will dominate your life during the year. For example, a Personal Year 1 is all about new beginnings and setting the stage for future growth, while a Personal Year 9 focuses on closure, reflection, and preparing for the next cycle.

Each year, the energy shifts, reflecting a different phase in the nine-year cycle of numerology. By calculating your Personal Year Number, you can align your actions and decisions with the natural flow of your life, making the most of each year's unique energy.

Understanding the Nine-Year Cycle in Numerology

In numerology, life is understood as a continuous cycle of growth, change, and renewal, with each phase lasting nine years. The nine-year cycle is a core concept in numerology, where each year is associated with a specific energy and focus. Understanding where you are in this cycle can help you navigate life more consciously, aligning your actions with the natural flow of events.

The cycle begins with **Personal Year 1**, which is a time of new beginnings. This year is about setting intentions, starting fresh projects, and taking the initiative. It's a year to focus on yourself and your goals, planting the seeds for what you want to achieve in the coming years.

Personal Year 2 is a year of cooperation, relationships, and patience. After the bold moves of Year 1, this year asks you to slow down, connect with others, and build strong foundations. It's a time for nurturing partnerships and developing emotional intelligence.

In **Personal Year 3**, the energy shifts toward creativity, self-expression, and social engagement. This is a year to explore your creative side, share your ideas with others, and enjoy the fruits of your earlier efforts. It's a time to be visible, sociable, and expressive.

Personal Year 4 brings a focus on stability, hard work, and building solid foundations. This year is about discipline, structure, and putting in the effort to create lasting results. It's a time to organize your life, manage your resources wisely, and set the stage for future success.

When you enter **Personal Year 5**, the focus turns to freedom, change, and adventure. This year is all about embracing new experiences, being adaptable, and stepping out of your comfort zone. It's a time for breaking free from routine and exploring new possibilities.

Personal Year 6 is centered around responsibility, family, and community. This is a year to focus on your relationships, take care of your loved ones, and create harmony in your home life. It's also a time for making commitments and nurturing those around you.

Personal Year 7 is a more introspective and spiritual year. It's a time for reflection, inner growth, and seeking deeper meaning in life. This year encourages you to focus on your inner world, perhaps through study, meditation, or spiritual practices.

In **Personal Year 8**, the energy shifts back to the external world, emphasizing power, success, and achievement. This is a year to focus on your career, financial goals, and personal ambitions. It's a time to step into leadership roles and manifest your desires into reality.

Finally, **Personal Year 9** marks the end of the cycle, bringing closure, reflection, and letting go. This is a year to wrap up loose ends, release what no longer serves you, and prepare for the new beginnings that will come with the next cycle. It's a time for forgiveness, compassion, and making peace with the past.

Understanding the nine-year cycle helps you see the bigger picture of your life, allowing you to align your actions with the energy of each year. By doing so, you can navigate your personal journey with greater awareness and purpose.

How Personal Year Numbers Affect Life Phases

Personal Year Numbers play a significant role in shaping the different phases of your life, guiding how you approach challenges, opportunities, and growth. Each year within the nine-year cycle carries its own energy, influencing the focus and direction of your life during that period. By understanding the impact of these numbers, you can make more informed decisions that align with the natural rhythm of your life.

For example, during a **Personal Year 1**, you are in a phase of new beginnings. This is a time to set the stage for future growth by starting new projects, making bold decisions, and embracing opportunities for personal development. The energy of Year 1 encourages you to take risks and pursue your goals with determination. For instance, if you've been considering launching a business or changing careers, this is the year to take action. The momentum you build during this year will influence the rest of the cycle.

As you move into a **Personal Year 2**, the focus shifts to relationships and collaboration. This phase emphasizes the importance of building connections, developing partnerships, and working harmoniously with others. It's a year to practice patience and diplomacy, making it ideal for resolving conflicts or strengthening your support network. If you've been working independently, this might be the time to seek out a mentor, collaborate with others, or deepen your personal relationships.

In a **Personal Year 3**, the emphasis is on creativity and self-expression. This phase encourages you to explore your artistic talents, communicate your ideas, and engage with the world in a more social and outgoing way. It's a time to share your thoughts, pursue hobbies, and connect with like-minded individuals. For example, if you've always wanted to write a book, start a blog, or take up painting, Year 3 provides the creative energy to do so.

During a **Personal Year 4**, the focus is on building a solid foundation. This phase is about discipline, organization, and hard work. It's a time to manage your resources wisely, plan for the future, and ensure that the groundwork is in place for long-term success. If you've been thinking about buying a home, starting a savings plan, or committing to a major project, this is the year to do it. The stability you create now will support you in the years to come.

In a **Personal Year 5**, change and adaptability take center stage. This phase is characterized by freedom, adventure, and the willingness to embrace new experiences. It's a time to break free from old patterns, explore new opportunities, and be open to the unexpected. Whether it's traveling to new places, learning a new skill, or making a significant lifestyle change, Year 5 provides the flexibility and courage to step into the unknown.

As you enter a **Personal Year 6**, the focus shifts to family, responsibility, and community. This phase emphasizes nurturing relationships, creating harmony in your home life, and taking on roles that require care and commitment. It's a time to focus on your loved ones, perhaps by resolving family issues, strengthening bonds, or taking on new responsibilities in your community.

In a **Personal Year 7**, introspection and spiritual growth become the focus. This phase encourages you to turn inward, seeking deeper understanding and personal growth. It's a time to explore your spiritual beliefs, engage in self-reflection, and pursue intellectual or philosophical interests. If you've been considering a period of study, meditation, or spiritual exploration, Year 7 provides the ideal environment for it.

During a **Personal Year 8**, the energy shifts back to achievement and material success. This phase is about power, ambition, and realizing your goals. It's a time to focus on your career, financial growth, and personal achievements. Whether it's seeking a promotion, expanding your business, or making significant financial investments, Year 8 supports your efforts to reach new heights.

Finally, in a **Personal Year 9**, the focus is on completion and letting go. This phase marks the end of the cycle, encouraging you to release what no longer serves you and prepare for new beginnings. It's a time to reflect on your journey, tie up loose ends, and make peace with the past. Whether it's ending a relationship, leaving a job, or or closing a chapter of your life, Year 9 allows you to release and renew, making space for the next cycle of growth and opportunity.

By embracing the energies of each Personal Year, you can navigate life's journey with greater clarity, purpose, and alignment with your soul's path.

CHAPTER 8: PINNACLE NUMBERS

What are Pinnacle Numbers?

Pinnacle Numbers in numerology represent significant phases in your life, each marked by specific energies and challenges that shape your personal development. These numbers reveal the themes and lessons you will encounter at different stages, providing insights into your growth and evolution over time.

Your life is divided into four Pinnacle Cycles, each influenced by a unique Pinnacle Number. These cycles are like chapters in a book, with each one building on the experiences and knowledge gained in the previous cycle. The Pinnacle Numbers are calculated using your full birth date, and each number reflects the opportunities, challenges, and areas of focus during that specific period.

To calculate your Pinnacle Numbers, you first break down your birth date into its individual components—day, month, and year. The four Pinnacle Numbers are derived as follows:

1. **First Pinnacle Number**: Add the month and day of your birth. For example, if you were born on March 15, you would add 3 (March) + 15 (1 + 5 = 6) to get 9. This is your First Pinnacle Number.
2. **Second Pinnacle Number**: Add the day and year of your birth. Using the same example, if you were born in 1990, you would add 15 (1 + 5 = 6) + 1990 (1 + 9 + 9 + 0 = 19, and 1 + 9 = 10, then 1 + 0 = 1) to get 6 + 1 = 7. This is your Second Pinnacle Number.
3. **Third Pinnacle Number**: Add the First and Second Pinnacle Numbers together. In this case, 9 + 7 = 16, and 1 + 6 = 7. So, the Third Pinnacle Number is 7.
4. **Fourth Pinnacle Number**: Add the month and year of your birth. Again, using March 15, 1990, you would add 3 (March) + 1990 (1 + 9 + 9 + 0 = 19, and 1 + 9 = 10, then 1 + 0 = 1) to get 3 + 1 = 4. This is your Fourth Pinnacle Number.

Each Pinnacle Number covers a specific period in your life, with the length of each cycle depending on your age. Typically, the First Pinnacle Cycle lasts until your early to mid-30s, the Second Pinnacle Cycle spans your 30s to late 40s, the Third Pinnacle Cycle covers your 50s and 60s, and the Fourth Pinnacle Cycle extends from your 60s onward.

The First Pinnacle Cycle often involves self-discovery and learning. This is a time when you explore who you are, your talents, and what you want from life. For example, if your First Pinnacle Number is 3, this period might be marked by creativity, communication, and self-expression. You might find yourself drawn to artistic pursuits, developing your communication skills, or engaging in social activities that allow you to express yourself.

The Second Pinnacle Cycle typically focuses on building and establishing your life's direction. If your Second Pinnacle Number is 8, this might be a period where you focus on career success, financial growth, and leadership roles. You might find yourself driven to achieve material goals, take on responsibilities, and solidify your place in the world.

The Third Pinnacle Cycle is often about refinement and mastery. If your Third Pinnacle Number is 6, this might be a time when you focus on family, community, and nurturing relationships. You may find fulfillment in taking care of others, creating a harmonious home environment, or contributing to your community in meaningful ways.

The Fourth Pinnacle Cycle is typically a time of reflection, wisdom, and legacy. If your Fourth Pinnacle Number is 9, this period might involve completing your life's work, giving back to others, and embracing a more spiritual or humanitarian outlook. You might feel a strong desire to leave a positive impact on the world, share your knowledge, and find peace in your achievements.

Understanding your Pinnacle Numbers can help you navigate each phase of your life with greater clarity and purpose. By aligning with the energy of your current Pinnacle Cycle, you can make the most of the opportunities and challenges that arise, leading to personal growth and fulfillment. Whether you're just starting out, building your life, refining your path, or reflecting on your journey, your Pinnacle Numbers offer insights into the unique experiences that shape your life.

Calculating Your Pinnacle Numbers

Calculating your Pinnacle Numbers in numerology involves using your full birth date to determine the four major cycles of your life. Each Pinnacle Number represents a specific phase in your life, characterized by particular energies, opportunities, and challenges that shape your personal development.

To calculate your Pinnacle Numbers, you first need to break down your birth date into its components: the month, day, and year of your birth. Here's a step-by-step guide on how to calculate each Pinnacle Number:

1. **First Pinnacle Number**: Add the digits of your birth month and day together.
    - Example: If you were born on April 16, calculate April as 4, and the day as 16 (1 + 6 = 7). Add these together: 4 + 7 = 11. If this is

a Master Number (11, 22, or 33), it remains as is. Otherwise, reduce it to a single digit by adding 1 + 1 = 2. So, the First Pinnacle Number is 2.

2. **Second Pinnacle Number**: Add the digits of your birth day and year together.
    ◦ Example: If you were born on April 16, 1985, calculate the day as 16 (1 + 6 = 7) and the year as 1985 (1 + 9 + 8 + 5 = 23, then 2 + 3 = 5). Add these together: 7 + 5 = 12, then reduce to a single digit: 1 + 2 = 3. So, the Second Pinnacle Number is 3.
3. **Third Pinnacle Number**: Add your First and Second Pinnacle Numbers together.
    ◦ Using the previous examples: 2 (First Pinnacle) + 3 (Second Pinnacle) = 5. So, the Third Pinnacle Number is 5.
4. **Fourth Pinnacle Number**: Add the digits of your birth month and year together.
    ◦ Using the same birth date: April (4) and 1985 (1 + 9 + 8 + 5 = 23, then 2 + 3 = 5). Add these together: 4 + 5 = 9. So, the Fourth Pinnacle Number is 9.

Each Pinnacle Number provides insight into the key themes of your life during that particular cycle. These numbers guide you through different stages of life, helping you understand the energies you're working with and how best to navigate them.

For example, if your First Pinnacle Number is 2, you may experience a period of focusing on relationships, cooperation, and diplomacy during the early part of your life. A Third Pinnacle Number of 5 might indicate a later phase in life characterized by change, freedom, and adventure. Understanding these numbers allows you to prepare for the challenges and opportunities that lie ahead, making the most of each phase.

The Four Pinnacle Phases in Life

The Four Pinnacle Phases in numerology represent distinct periods in your life, each governed by a specific Pinnacle Number. These phases serve as guideposts, marking key chapters of personal growth, challenges, and achievements. Each phase offers different opportunities and lessons that align with your overall life path.

First Pinnacle Phase: This phase typically covers the early years of your life, from birth until your early 30s. It's a time of self-discovery and laying the foundation for your future. The First Pinnacle Number indicates the energies that will shape this period. For example, if your First Pinnacle Number is 1, this phase might be characterized by independence, ambition, and a strong drive to establish yourself. You might find yourself taking bold steps, exploring new territories, and setting the stage for your future successes.

Second Pinnacle Phase: The Second Pinnacle Phase usually spans your 30s and 40s, a time when you're likely building and solidifying your life's direction. This phase often involves career development, relationships, and establishing a stable foundation. If your Second Pinnacle Number is 4, this period may focus on hard work, discipline, and creating structure in your life. You might be driven to achieve stability in your career, finances, and home life, laying down the groundwork for long-term success.

Third Pinnacle Phase: The Third Pinnacle Phase covers the years from your 50s to late 60s, a time often associated with refinement and mastery. This phase is about reaping the rewards of your earlier efforts and focusing on personal fulfillment. For instance, if your Third Pinnacle Number is 6, this might be a period where family, community, and nurturing relationships take center stage. You may find yourself dedicating more time to loved ones, contributing to your community, and focusing on creating a harmonious environment.

Fourth Pinnacle Phase: The Fourth Pinnacle Phase begins in your late 60s and continues for the rest of your life. This final phase is often about reflection, wisdom, and leaving a legacy. The energies of your Fourth Pinnacle Number guide how you conclude your life's journey. If your Fourth Pinnacle Number is 9, this phase might be characterized by a focus on humanitarian efforts, compassion, and spiritual growth. You may feel a strong urge to give back, share your wisdom, and make a positive impact on the world.

Each Pinnacle Phase builds upon the previous one, creating a progression of experiences and growth. For example, a person with a First Pinnacle Number of 3 might spend their early years exploring creative pursuits and self-expression. If their Second Pinnacle Number is 8, they might shift their focus in their 30s and 40s to career success and material achievement. As they enter the Third Pinnacle Phase, a 6 might lead them to prioritize family and community, with the Fourth Pinnacle Number of 9 guiding them toward a legacy of compassion and service.

Understanding these phases allows you to navigate your life with greater awareness, making the most of each stage's unique opportunities and challenges.

Using Pinnacle Numbers for Long-Term Planning

Pinnacle Numbers in numerology are not just tools for understanding the different phases of your life; they are also valuable for long-term planning. By aligning your life goals and decisions with the energies of your Pinnacle Numbers, you can create a roadmap that leads to personal fulfillment and success.

When you know your Pinnacle Numbers, you gain insights into the focus areas for each stage of your life. This allows you to plan ahead, making choices that align with the energies you'll be working with at different times.

For example, if your Second Pinnacle Number is 4, you know that your 30s and 40s will be a time for building stability, structure, and discipline in your life. Knowing this, you can prioritize long-term goals during this period, such as buying a home, advancing in your career, or establishing a solid financial foundation. You might focus on making decisions that require careful planning and a methodical approach, ensuring that you are laying the groundwork for future security.

On the other hand, if your Third Pinnacle Number is 5, you can anticipate that your 50s and 60s will be characterized by change, freedom, and adventure. During this phase, you might plan for activities that allow you to explore new horizons, whether that's through travel, learning new skills, or embracing new opportunities. Understanding that this phase is about flexibility and adaptability can help you prepare for a more dynamic and less predictable period of life.

For those with a Fourth Pinnacle Number of 9, long-term planning might involve focusing on leaving a legacy and contributing to the greater good. As you approach your later years, you might prioritize philanthropic activities, mentoring, or sharing your knowledge and experience with others. Planning for this phase could involve creating a foundation, writing a book, or engaging in humanitarian efforts that reflect your values and ideals.

Using Pinnacle Numbers for long-term planning also helps you make sense of the transitions between different life phases. For instance, moving from a Second Pinnacle Number of 2, which emphasizes relationships and partnerships, to a Third Pinnacle Number of 7, which focuses on introspection and spiritual growth, might require a shift in priorities. By anticipating this transition, you can prepare to spend more time on personal development, study, or spiritual practices as you move into the next phase of life.

Additionally, understanding your Pinnacle Numbers can guide you in setting realistic and meaningful goals. For example, if you know that your Fourth Pinnacle Phase is likely to be focused on service and compassion (with a Pinnacle Number of 9), you can plan to gradually shift your focus from material achievements to more altruistic endeavors. This can help you create a life plan that evolves naturally, reflecting your personal growth and changing priorities over time.

In essence, using Pinnacle Numbers for long-term planning allows you to align your life path with the natural rhythms and energies of your numerology chart. By doing so, you can make informed decisions that support your personal growth, ensuring that each phase of your life is fulfilling and purposeful. Whether you're planning for the next decade or considering your legacy, Pinnacle Numbers provide a valuable framework for shaping your future.

CHAPTER 9: CHALLENGE NUMBERS

Understanding Challenge Numbers

Challenge Numbers in numerology reveal the specific obstacles and difficulties you are likely to encounter at different stages of your life. These numbers help you understand the areas where you may face internal or external challenges, guiding you to develop the strengths and resilience needed to overcome them.

Each person has four Challenge Numbers, corresponding to different phases of life. These challenges are not meant to be seen as negative forces, but rather as opportunities for growth and self-improvement. Understanding your Challenge Numbers allows you to anticipate potential difficulties and prepare yourself to navigate them more effectively.

How to Calculate Your Challenge Numbers

Challenge Numbers are calculated using the digits of your birth date. To find your Challenge Numbers, you subtract the digits of your birth month, day, and year from each other in specific combinations. The process involves a few steps:

1. **First Challenge Number**: Subtract the digits of your birth day from the digits of your birth month.
    - Example: If you were born on March 15, calculate March as 3 and 15 as 6 (1 + 5). Subtract 3 from 6: 6 - 3 = 3. So, the First Challenge Number is 3.
2. **Second Challenge Number**: Subtract the digits of your birth day from the digits of your birth year.
    - Example: Using the birth date March 15, 1990, first reduce the year to a single digit: 1 + 9 + 9 + 0 = 19, and 1 + 9 = 10, then 1 + 0 = 1. Subtract the birth day (6) from the year (1): 6 - 1 = 5. The Second Challenge Number is 5.
3. **Third Challenge Number**: Subtract the digits of your birth month from the digits of your birth year.
    - Using the same birth date: March (3) and 1990 (1). Subtract 1 from 3: 3 - 1 = 2. The Third Challenge Number is 2.
4. **Fourth Challenge Number**: This is calculated by subtracting your First Challenge Number from your Third Challenge Number.
    - From the above examples: 3 (First Challenge) and 2 (Third Challenge). Subtract 2 from 3: 3 - 2 = 1. So, the Fourth Challenge Number is 1.

The Four Challenge Phases

Each Challenge Number corresponds to a specific phase in your life:

1. **First Challenge**: This usually covers your early years, up to around age 30. The First Challenge often involves discovering your identity and dealing with the initial struggles of finding your place in the world. For example, if your First Challenge Number is 3, you might face difficulties related to communication and self-expression. You may need to work on developing confidence in sharing your thoughts and ideas.
2. **Second Challenge**: This phase generally spans from your 30s to mid-40s. During this time, you might be dealing with the responsibilities of career, family, and personal growth. A Second Challenge Number of 5 could indicate challenges related to freedom and change. You might struggle with balancing the need for independence with the demands of stability and commitment.
3. **Third Challenge**: This phase typically occurs in your mid-40s to late 50s. It's a time when you are refining your life's work and preparing for the later stages of life. If your Third Challenge Number is 2, you might face difficulties in relationships, requiring you to develop patience, diplomacy, and cooperation.
4. **Fourth Challenge**: This final phase begins around your late 50s and continues for the rest of your life. The Fourth Challenge is about integrating the lessons learned throughout your life and finding peace and fulfillment. A Fourth Challenge Number of 1 might suggest struggles with independence and self-reliance, indicating that you need to focus on maintaining your sense of self as you age.

How to Calculate Your Challenge Numbers

Challenge Numbers in numerology are derived from your birth date and reveal the specific obstacles and difficulties you are likely to encounter at different stages of your life. These numbers help you understand where you may face internal or external challenges, offering insights into the areas where you need to grow and develop. Calculating your Challenge Numbers involves a simple process using the digits of your birth date.

Here's how to calculate each of your four Challenge Numbers:

1. **First Challenge Number**: Subtract the digits of your birth day from the digits of your birth month.
    - Example: If you were born on July 14, you would calculate July as 7 and 14 as 1 + 4 = 5. Subtract these: 7 - 5 = 2. So, your First Challenge Number is 2.
2. **Second Challenge Number**: Subtract the digits of your birth day from the digits of your birth year.

- Example: For the same birth date in 1987, first reduce the year: 1 + 9 + 8 + 7 = 25, and then 2 + 5 = 7. Now, subtract the birth day (5) from the year (7): 7 - 5 = 2. This makes your Second Challenge Number 2.
3. **Third Challenge Number**: Subtract the digits of your birth month from the digits of your birth year.
    - Using the same example: Subtract the month (7) from the year (7): 7 - 7 = 0. If the result is 0, your Third Challenge Number is 0, which suggests unique challenges related to all numbers and requires balancing various aspects of life.
4. **Fourth Challenge Number**: Subtract your First Challenge Number from your Second Challenge Number.
    - Continuing the example: Subtract the First Challenge Number (2) from the Second Challenge Number (2): 2 - 2 = 0. Again, if the result is 0, this is a sign of a complex, multifaceted challenge.

These Challenge Numbers correspond to different phases of your life and provide clues about the types of difficulties you might face during each phase.

- The **First Challenge** typically covers your early years, up to about age 30.
- The **Second Challenge** spans the period from your 30s to mid-40s.
- The **Third Challenge** generally occurs from your mid-40s to late 50s.
- The **Fourth Challenge** begins in your late 50s and continues for the rest of your life.

Understanding these numbers can help you prepare for and navigate the specific challenges that arise in each phase of life.

Interpreting the Impact of Challenge Numbers

Challenge Numbers in numerology are key to understanding the specific obstacles you may encounter throughout your life. These numbers highlight areas where you might struggle, providing insight into the underlying issues you need to address to achieve personal growth.

Each Challenge Number, ranging from 0 to 9, has its own unique influence:

- **Challenge Number 1**: This number suggests struggles with self-confidence, independence, and leadership. You might find it difficult to assert yourself, often doubting your capabilities. The impact of this challenge could be felt in situations where you need to take the lead or make decisions. For example, you might shy away from opportunities that require you to be in charge, which could limit your career growth.

- **Challenge Number 2**: A Challenge Number 2 indicates difficulties with relationships, cooperation, and sensitivity. You might struggle with being overly sensitive or finding it hard to work well with others. This challenge could manifest in personal or professional relationships, where you might find it difficult to maintain harmony or avoid conflicts.
- **Challenge Number 3**: If your Challenge Number is 3, you may face issues with communication, self-expression, and creativity. You might find it challenging to convey your thoughts and feelings, leading to misunderstandings or missed opportunities. This challenge can impact your ability to build strong connections with others or fully express your creative potential.
- **Challenge Number 4**: A Challenge Number 4 suggests struggles with discipline, organization, and stability. You might find it hard to stay focused, manage your time effectively, or create a stable foundation in your life. This challenge could lead to feelings of frustration or insecurity, especially in areas that require long-term commitment or careful planning.
- **Challenge Number 5**: With a Challenge Number 5, you might struggle with change, freedom, and adaptability. You may find it difficult to adjust to new situations or feel restless and dissatisfied with routines. This challenge can affect your ability to maintain consistency in your life, leading to frequent changes in direction or difficulty in staying committed to your goals.
- **Challenge Number 6**: If you have a Challenge Number 6, you might face issues with responsibility, family, and balance. You may struggle with taking on too much responsibility or finding it hard to say no, leading to feelings of overwhelm. This challenge could impact your relationships with family and loved ones, where you might feel pressured to meet others' expectations at the expense of your own needs.
- **Challenge Number 7**: A Challenge Number 7 indicates difficulties with introspection, spirituality, and trust. You might struggle with connecting to your inner self or trusting your intuition. This challenge can lead to feelings of isolation or confusion, especially in situations where you need to rely on your inner guidance.
- **Challenge Number 8**: If your Challenge Number is 8, you may face issues with power, authority, and material success. You might struggle with asserting yourself in positions of power or managing your resources effectively. This challenge could lead to difficulties in achieving your goals or dealing with issues related to control and ambition.
- **Challenge Number 9**: A Challenge Number 9 suggests struggles with compassion, idealism, and letting go. You might find it hard to release the past or to fully embrace your humanitarian instincts. This challenge can lead to feelings of frustration or disappointment, especially when your ideals clash with reality.

Interpreting your Challenge Numbers allows you to identify the specific areas where you need to focus your efforts. By understanding the impact of these numbers, you can develop strategies to overcome your challenges and grow in those areas.

Strategies for Overcoming Challenges in Numerology

Overcoming the challenges indicated by your Challenge Numbers in numerology requires a proactive and mindful approach. These challenges highlight specific areas where you may face difficulties, but they also provide opportunities for personal growth and self-improvement. By understanding and addressing these challenges, you can turn potential obstacles into strengths.

For a Challenge Number 1, the focus is on building self-confidence and leadership skills. To overcome this challenge, start by taking small steps to assert yourself in everyday situations. Practice decision-making and take on roles that require you to lead, even if they are minor. Gradually, you'll build the confidence needed to handle larger responsibilities. Surround yourself with supportive individuals who encourage your growth, and seek out opportunities that allow you to demonstrate your capabilities.

With a Challenge Number 2, the key is to develop stronger relationship skills and emotional resilience. Work on improving your communication abilities, particularly in listening and responding to others with empathy. Practice patience in your interactions and learn to value collaboration over competition. Engaging in activities that promote teamwork, such as group projects or community service, can help you build trust and cooperation with others.

For a Challenge Number 3, overcoming difficulties with self-expression and creativity involves finding your voice. Engage in creative activities that allow you to express yourself, such as writing, art, or public speaking. Practice articulating your thoughts and feelings clearly, both in personal and professional settings. Joining groups or classes that focus on communication skills can also help you become more comfortable with expressing yourself.

If you have a Challenge Number 4, the focus should be on developing discipline and organizational skills. Start by creating structured routines in your daily life, such as setting regular goals and deadlines. Break larger tasks into manageable steps to avoid feeling overwhelmed. Practice time management techniques and prioritize your responsibilities to ensure that you stay on track. Building a solid foundation in your life requires consistent effort, so be patient with your progress.

With a Challenge Number 5, the key to overcoming restlessness and a desire for constant change is to find a balance between freedom and commitment. Embrace new experiences while also recognizing the value of stability. Set goals that allow for flexibility but also require long-term dedication. Learning to adapt to change without losing focus on your objectives is crucial. Engage in activities that satisfy your need for variety while also providing a sense of purpose and direction.

For a Challenge Number 6, balancing responsibility with self-care is essential. Learn to set boundaries and say no when necessary to avoid taking on too much. Focus on creating harmony in your relationships by communicating openly and honestly with loved ones. Practice self-care and ensure that you're meeting your own needs, even as you care for others. Finding a balance between giving and receiving will help you overcome feelings of overwhelm.

If you have a Challenge Number 7, overcoming difficulties with introspection and spirituality involves deepening your connection to your inner self. Engage in practices that promote self-awareness, such as meditation, journaling, or quiet reflection. Trust your intuition and learn to listen to your inner guidance. Seek out spiritual or philosophical teachings that resonate with you, and explore them in a way that feels meaningful.

For a Challenge Number 8, overcoming struggles with power and authority requires developing a healthy relationship with ambition and success. Focus on setting realistic goals and managing your resources wisely. Practice asserting yourself in a balanced way, without resorting to control or manipulation. Learn to recognize and appreciate your achievements, but also understand the importance of using your power for the greater good.

With a Challenge Number 9, the key to overcoming difficulties with compassion and letting go is to practice forgiveness and release. Work on releasing past hurts and embracing the present moment. Practice self-compassion and recognize that holding onto grudges only holds you back. Engage in activities that promote emotional release, such as writing, art, or talking to a trusted friend. Learn to let go of attachments to outcomes and trust that everything is working in your favor. By releasing the past and embracing forgiveness, you'll be able to move forward with greater ease and compassion, creating space for new experiences and relationships to emerge. Remember, overcoming your Challenge Number is a journey, and patience, self-awareness, and kindness are your greatest allies.

CHAPTER 10: KARMIC NUMBERS

Introduction to Karmic Debt Numbers

Karmic Debt Numbers in numerology represent specific lessons that an individual is believed to carry from past actions, often from previous lifetimes. These numbers highlight the challenges and issues that need to be addressed and resolved in this lifetime. The concept of Karmic Debt is rooted in the idea that actions from the past, particularly those that were harmful or unbalanced, create an energetic debt that must be repaid through life experiences.

There are four main Karmic Debt Numbers: 13, 14, 16, and 19. Each of these numbers is associated with a specific type of karmic lesson, reflecting the nature of the past actions that created the debt. Understanding your Karmic Debt Number can provide insights into the recurring challenges in your life and guide you toward personal growth and balance.

Karmic Debt Number 13

The Karmic Debt Number 13 is often associated with the lesson of hard work and discipline. In past actions, there may have been an avoidance of responsibility, laziness, or a tendency to take shortcuts at the expense of others. As a result, individuals with this Karmic Debt are often required to develop a strong work ethic and to approach their responsibilities with dedication and focus.

For example, someone with Karmic Debt 13 might find that they repeatedly face situations where they need to work harder than others to achieve the same results. This can be frustrating, but it serves as a reminder to embrace discipline and perseverance. By meeting challenges head-on and avoiding the temptation to cut corners, they can clear this karmic debt and build a solid foundation for future success.

Karmic Debt Number 14

The Karmic Debt Number 14 is connected to issues of freedom, self-control, and balance. In past actions, there may have been abuse of freedom, such as excessive indulgence in physical pleasures or an inability to manage one's desires responsibly. This number calls for the individual to learn how to balance personal freedom with responsibility, developing self-discipline and making wise choices.

An individual with Karmic Debt 14 may find that their life is marked by periods of instability, with sudden changes and disruptions that force them to learn how to maintain equilibrium. They might struggle with addictions or find it difficult to stay committed to long-term goals. The lesson here is to cultivate inner strength and to use freedom constructively rather than destructively.

Karmic Debt Number 16

Karmic Debt Number 16 relates to the lesson of ego and humility. In past actions, there may have been an overemphasis on the self, arrogance, or a disregard for others. The presence of this number suggests that the individual must learn the importance of humility and the dangers of allowing ego to dominate their life.

Those with Karmic Debt 16 often experience situations where their ego is challenged, leading to a humbling process that forces them to reassess their priorities. This can manifest as the sudden loss of status, relationships, or material wealth, which serves as a wake-up call to focus on spiritual growth and self-awareness. The path to clearing this debt involves embracing humility, recognizing the interconnectedness of all life, and developing a genuine sense of service to others.

Karmic Debt Number 19

The Karmic Debt Number 19 is linked to the theme of independence and power. In past actions, there may have been an abuse of power or a tendency to manipulate others for personal gain. The lesson associated with this number is to learn how to use personal power responsibly and to develop a sense of true independence without exploiting others.

Individuals with Karmic Debt 19 may find themselves in situations where they must stand on their own, often without the support they might have taken for granted in the past. This can be a lonely and challenging path, but it teaches the importance of self-reliance and the ethical use of power. To clear this debt, they must learn to lead with integrity, respect the autonomy of others, and build their success through honest and fair means.

Recognizing and Working with Karmic Debt Numbers

Understanding your Karmic Debt Number can be a powerful tool for personal growth. It helps you recognize the recurring challenges and patterns in your life that may stem from unresolved issues in the past. By consciously working through these challenges, you can transform the energy of your Karmic Debt into positive growth and clear the path for a more balanced and fulfilling life.

For instance, if you discover that you have a Karmic Debt Number 16, you might reflect on moments when pride or ego led to difficulties in your relationships or career. Recognizing this pattern allows you to take deliberate steps toward humility and self-awareness, thereby neutralizing the negative effects of the karmic debt.

Each Karmic Debt Number serves as a guide, pointing out where growth is needed and offering a roadmap for overcoming the obstacles that stand in the way of your full potential. By addressing these karmic lessons with mindfulness and intention, you can break free from past patterns and create a more harmonious future.

The Significance of Karmic Lessons

Karmic lessons in numerology represent unresolved issues from past lives or earlier in this life that have carried over to your current experience. These lessons highlight areas where growth, understanding, and healing are needed. The significance of karmic lessons lies in their ability to guide you toward a more balanced and fulfilled life by addressing the challenges and patterns that might otherwise hold you back.

Karmic lessons often manifest as recurring challenges or patterns in your life. For example, if you repeatedly encounter difficulties in relationships, this could indicate a karmic lesson around understanding, empathy, or communication. The universe presents these challenges as opportunities for growth, encouraging you to learn from your experiences and break free from limiting patterns.

One common karmic lesson revolves around the concept of balance. If, in a past life, you focused excessively on material wealth at the expense of relationships, you might find yourself in this lifetime struggling to maintain financial stability while fostering meaningful connections. This lesson teaches you to balance your material pursuits with emotional and spiritual fulfillment, ensuring that you don't neglect one aspect of life for the sake of another.

Another significant karmic lesson involves power and control. Suppose you misused power or manipulated others in a previous life. In that case, you might face situations in this life where you feel powerless or are subjected to the control of others. The lesson here is to learn how to use power responsibly and ethically, recognizing the importance of mutual respect and cooperation.

The significance of karmic lessons also extends to self-awareness and personal growth. By recognizing the areas in which you need to grow, you can actively work to transform these challenges into strengths. For instance, if you have a karmic lesson related to independence, you might struggle with relying too heavily on others or feel overly responsible for their well-being. Understanding this lesson allows you to cultivate healthy boundaries and develop a stronger sense of self-reliance.

Karmic lessons are not about punishment but about growth and evolution. They offer you the chance to correct imbalances from the past and move forward with greater wisdom and understanding. By addressing these lessons with an open heart and a willingness to learn, you can create a more harmonious and fulfilling life.

Ultimately, the significance of karmic lessons lies in their potential to transform your life. They challenge you to confront your limitations, learn from your experiences, and evolve into a more balanced and conscious individual. By embracing these lessons, you not only heal the past but also pave the way for a brighter and more empowered future.

Identifying Karmic Numbers in Your Chart

Karmic Numbers in numerology reveal specific lessons that you are meant to address in this lifetime. These numbers point to areas where you might have unresolved issues from the past, often carrying over from previous lives. Identifying Karmic Numbers in your chart helps you understand the challenges you face and the lessons you need to learn to achieve balance and growth.

In numerology, certain numbers are considered Karmic Debt Numbers: 13, 14, 16, and 19. These numbers suggest that there is a karmic imbalance from a past life that needs to be addressed. To identify these numbers in your chart, you need to calculate key elements such as your Life Path Number, Destiny Number, and Expression Number. If any of these numbers reduce to 13, 14, 16, or 19, it indicates a karmic debt.

For example, if your birth date is November 3, 1986, your Life Path Number is calculated by adding the digits together: $1 + 1 + 3 + 1 + 9 + 8 + 6 = 29$, and then $2 + 9 = 11$. Since 11 is a Master Number, it does not reduce further, and it does not indicate a karmic debt. However, if your Life Path Number were to reduce to 13, 14, 16, or 19, it would indicate that you have a specific karmic lesson to address.

Another way to identify Karmic Numbers is by examining your name. In numerology, each letter of your name corresponds to a specific number. By calculating the total for your name, you can determine whether any Karmic Numbers appear. For example, if your name calculation results in a total of 16, this would indicate a karmic debt related to issues of ego and humility.

Additionally, Karmic Numbers can appear in the Pinnacle and Challenge Numbers of your numerology chart. These elements indicate the specific periods in your life where karmic lessons will be most prominent. For instance, if you have a Pinnacle Number of 14, you may face challenges related to freedom and self-control during that particular phase of your life.

Identifying Karmic Numbers in your chart provides a roadmap for understanding the lessons you need to learn. It offers insights into the recurring patterns and challenges you may face, allowing you to approach them with greater awareness and intention. For example, if you identify that you have a Karmic Number of 19 in your chart, you can work on developing healthy independence and ethical leadership, knowing that this is a key area of growth for you.

Understanding where these Karmic Numbers appear in your chart helps you recognize the underlying issues that may be influencing your life. By addressing these karmic debts consciously, you can work toward resolving them, leading to a more balanced and fulfilling life.

How to Address and Balance Karmic Debt

Addressing and balancing Karmic Debt in numerology involves recognizing the specific lessons associated with your Karmic Numbers and taking intentional steps to resolve these challenges. Karmic Debt is not a punishment but an opportunity for growth, offering you the chance to correct past imbalances and move forward with greater wisdom and understanding.

The first step in addressing Karmic Debt is to identify the Karmic Numbers in your chart, such as 13, 14, 16, or 19. Each of these numbers corresponds to a specific type of karmic lesson. For example, the Karmic Debt Number 13 is associated with lessons around hard work, discipline, and responsibility. If you have this number in your chart, you may need to focus on developing a strong work ethic and avoiding shortcuts that could lead to further imbalances.

Once you've identified your Karmic Debt Number, the next step is to understand the underlying issues and patterns associated with it. For instance, if you have Karmic Debt Number 14, the lesson revolves around finding a balance between freedom and responsibility. You may need to work on controlling impulsive behavior, managing your desires responsibly, and maintaining a sense of balance in your life.

To address and balance Karmic Debt, it's important to adopt practices and behaviors that align with the lessons you need to learn. For example, if you have Karmic Debt Number 16, which is related to issues of ego and humility, you might focus on cultivating humility and self-awareness. This could involve practices such as meditation, self-reflection, and seeking feedback from others to help you stay grounded and aware of your impact on those around you.

Another key aspect of balancing Karmic Debt is to consciously make choices that counteract the negative patterns associated with your Karmic Numbers. For example, if you have Karmic Debt Number 19, which is linked to independence and power, you might need to focus on using your power responsibly and ethically. This could involve being more considerate of others' needs, avoiding manipulative behavior, and striving to build relationships based on mutual respect and trust.

In addition to behavioral changes, addressing Karmic Debt often involves inner work. This might include exploring the emotional and psychological roots of your challenges, seeking therapy or counseling to work through past traumas, or engaging in spiritual practices that help you connect with your higher self. For example, if you struggle with Karmic Debt related to self-control (associated with Karmic Number 14), you might benefit from mindfulness practices that help you become more aware of your impulses and develop greater self-discipline.

Balancing Karmic Debt also requires patience and persistence. These lessons are often deeply ingrained and may take time to fully understand and resolve. It's important to approach this work with compassion for yourself, recognizing that growth is a gradual process. Each step you take toward resolving your Karmic Debt brings you closer to a more balanced and fulfilling life.

Finally, consider how you can integrate these lessons into your daily life. For example, if your Karmic Debt involves issues of responsibility (as with Karmic Debt 13), you might commit to taking on tasks and roles that challenge you to be more disciplined and reliable. By consistently practicing these behaviors, you can gradually transform the energy of your Karmic Debt into positive growth, leading to greater harmony and balance in your life.

CHAPTER 11: MASTER NUMBERS

Interpreting Master Numbers 11, 22, and 33

In numerology, Master Numbers 11, 22, and 33 are considered the most powerful and spiritually significant numbers. They are not reduced to single digits because they carry higher vibrational energies and more profound lessons. These numbers represent a higher level of spiritual awareness, intuition, and purpose. However, they also come with greater responsibilities and challenges. Understanding these numbers in your numerology chart can provide deep insights into your life path and purpose.

Master Number 11 is often referred to as the "Spiritual Messenger" or "Illuminator." It is associated with intuition, spiritual insight, and a deep connection to the subconscious mind. People with Master Number 11 in their chart are often highly intuitive and sensitive, with a natural ability to perceive things that others might miss. They may feel a strong calling to inspire others, whether through teaching, healing, or creative expression.

For example, someone with a Life Path Number 11 might find themselves drawn to careers or activities that involve guiding others toward spiritual or personal growth. They may have a deep interest in the metaphysical, psychology, or arts, using their intuitive gifts to bring light to others. However, the energy of 11 can also lead to feelings of anxiety or nervousness, as the person may struggle to balance their heightened sensitivity with the demands of the physical world.

Master Number 22 is known as the "Master Builder." It represents the ability to turn dreams into reality through practical, methodical work. People with this number are often visionaries who can see the big picture and have the practical skills to bring their ideas to life. They are highly ambitious and have the potential to achieve great things, often in ways that benefit others on a large scale.

For instance, a person with a Destiny Number 22 might be driven to build something lasting, whether it's a business, a social movement, or a physical structure. They have a strong sense of purpose and the capability to manifest their goals into tangible results. However, the energy of 22 can also lead to immense pressure, as they may feel burdened by the responsibility of their potential. Balancing the spiritual and material aspects of their life is crucial for someone with this Master Number.

Master Number 33 is often called the "Master Teacher." It is the number of the compassionate healer, someone who is dedicated to raising the consciousness of humanity. This number embodies the energies of unconditional love, selflessness, and service to others. People with Master Number 33 are often driven by a desire to make the world a better place, often through teaching, healing, or spiritual leadership.

For example, an individual with an Expression Number 33 might feel compelled to work in fields such as counseling, teaching, or humanitarian efforts. They are natural nurturers, with a deep capacity for empathy and a strong desire to alleviate the suffering of others. However, the energy of 33 can also be overwhelming, as they may struggle with maintaining their own well-being while giving so much to others. Learning to balance their self-care with their desire to serve is essential for those with this Master Number.

Master Numbers 11, 22, and 33 are often seen as rare gifts, but they require a high level of awareness and responsibility to fully realize their potential. Individuals with these numbers in their chart are called to rise to a higher level of consciousness and to use their gifts to benefit others. Understanding the unique energies and challenges associated with these numbers can help them navigate their life path with greater clarity and purpose.

The Higher Vibration and Challenges of Master Numbers

Master Numbers 11, 22, and 33 are known for their higher vibrations, which bring both extraordinary potential and significant challenges. These numbers are considered to carry spiritual and cosmic energy that transcends the typical influence of single-digit numbers. However, living up to the high expectations associated with Master Numbers requires dedication, balance, and self-awareness.

The **higher vibration** of Master Number 11 is closely linked to spiritual enlightenment and intuitive insight. Individuals with this number often possess a heightened sensitivity to the energies around them, which can lead to profound spiritual experiences and a deep connection with the metaphysical world. They may have vivid dreams, strong gut feelings, or an innate understanding of the underlying truths in life. This intuitive power enables them to be powerful communicators, artists, and healers, capable of inspiring and guiding others.

However, the challenges associated with Master Number 11 stem from this same sensitivity. The intense energy of 11 can lead to feelings of anxiety, nervousness, or overwhelm, as the individual may struggle to process the constant influx of emotions and insights. Balancing their inner world with the demands of everyday life is crucial. For example, someone with a Life Path Number 11 might find it difficult to ground themselves, leading to periods of self-doubt or confusion. Practicing mindfulness, meditation, or other grounding techniques can help them channel their energy positively.

Master Number 22 vibrates with the energy of practical manifestation. It is often seen as the most powerful of all the numbers because it combines the spiritual insight of the number 11 with the practical, grounded energy of the number 4. This makes 22 a "Master Builder," capable of turning grand visions into reality. Individuals with this number are often highly ambitious, with a strong drive to achieve their goals and create something of lasting value.

The challenge for those with Master Number 22 lies in the pressure to live up to their potential. The expectations placed on them, whether by themselves or others, can be immense. They may feel burdened by the responsibility of their abilities, leading to stress or burnout. For example, someone with a Destiny Number 22 might take on too many projects or responsibilities, trying to do it all, which can lead to exhaustion. Learning to delegate, prioritize, and maintain a healthy work-life balance is essential for harnessing the full power of this number.

Master Number 33 carries the vibration of universal love and selfless service. It is considered the "Master Teacher" and is associated with compassion, empathy, and the desire to help others. People with this number are often deeply committed to making a positive impact on the world, whether through teaching, healing, or humanitarian work. They have a natural ability to uplift and inspire those around them, often becoming role models or leaders in their communities.

The challenge for those with Master Number 33 is the potential for self-sacrifice. The intense desire to help others can lead to neglecting their own needs, resulting in burnout or emotional exhaustion. For instance, an individual with an Expression Number 33 might constantly put others first, leading to a lack of self-care and eventually, resentment or fatigue. These individuals must learn the importance of self-love and boundaries, ensuring that they maintain their own well-being while serving others.

Incorporating Master Numbers into Daily Life

Master Numbers 11, 22, and 33 are powerful influences in numerology, representing heightened spiritual energies and unique challenges. While these numbers bring extraordinary potential, integrating their energy into daily life requires conscious effort and mindful practices. By aligning your everyday actions with the qualities of your Master Number, you can live more harmoniously and effectively harness the power these numbers offer.

For those with Master Number 11, the focus is on intuition, inspiration, and spiritual insight. Incorporating the energy of 11 into your daily life involves paying close attention to your inner voice and intuition. Start each day with a practice that connects you to your inner self, such as meditation or journaling. This helps you tune in to the subtle messages and guidance that your intuition provides. For instance, you might use your intuitive insights to navigate decisions at work or in your personal life, trusting that your inner wisdom will lead you in the right direction.

Another way to integrate the energy of 11 is through creative expression. Since Master Number 11 is often linked to artistic and spiritual creativity, finding outlets for these expressions in your daily routine can be incredibly fulfilling. Whether it's through writing, painting, music, or other forms of art, regularly engaging in creative activities allows you to channel the high vibrations of 11 into something tangible and meaningful.

If you have Master Number 22, your focus is on building and manifesting your dreams into reality. This number is associated with practical mastery, combining visionary thinking with a grounded approach to life. To incorporate the energy of 22 into your daily routine, start by setting clear, actionable goals. Break down your long-term visions into manageable steps that you can work on every day. For example, if you're working on a large project, make a habit of tackling a small portion of it each day, steadily building toward your ultimate goal.

Another important aspect of Master Number 22 is balance. Given the immense potential and responsibility associated with this number, it's crucial to maintain a healthy work-life balance. Incorporate regular self-care practices into your daily routine to ensure that you stay grounded and focused. This might include physical exercise, spending time in nature, or simply taking time out for relaxation and reflection.

For those with Master Number 33, the focus is on compassion, healing, and service to others. This number embodies the qualities of the "Master Teacher," emphasizing the importance of nurturing and guiding others. To bring the energy of 33 into your daily life, look for opportunities to help and support those around you. This can be as simple as offering a kind word to a colleague, volunteering in your community, or providing emotional support to a friend in need.

Additionally, incorporating the energy of 33 involves practicing self-compassion. As someone who is naturally inclined to give to others, it's essential to ensure that you're also taking care of your own needs. Start your day with affirmations of self-love, or incorporate a daily ritual that nourishes your body, mind, and spirit. This balance between giving and receiving is key to living harmoniously with the energy of 33.

Incorporating Master Numbers into daily life is about aligning your actions with the unique qualities of these numbers. Whether through intuition, practical building, or compassionate service, living in harmony with your Master Number helps you fulfill your potential and make a positive impact on the world around you.

Master Numbers in Spiritual Development

Master Numbers 11, 22, and 33 hold significant spiritual energy, often guiding individuals toward higher levels of consciousness and spiritual growth. Integrating these numbers into your spiritual development involves recognizing the unique spiritual lessons and challenges each number presents and using them as a framework for personal and spiritual evolution.

Master Number 11 is closely associated with spiritual enlightenment, intuition, and a deep connection to the metaphysical world. For those with this number, spiritual development often involves cultivating a strong sense of inner awareness and trust in one's intuition. Engaging in practices like meditation, mindfulness, and dream work can help you tap into the spiritual insights that the number 11 offers. For example, you might start a daily meditation practice focused on connecting with your higher self, seeking guidance, and gaining clarity on your spiritual path.

Spiritual development for those with Master Number 11 also involves learning to balance the intense energies of this number. The heightened sensitivity that comes with 11 can sometimes lead to feelings of overwhelm or anxiety. Therefore, grounding practices, such as spending time in nature, engaging in physical activity, or using grounding crystals, can be beneficial. These practices help stabilize the spiritual energy of 11, making it easier to navigate the challenges that come with heightened intuition and awareness.

Master Number 22 is often called the "Master Builder" because it combines the visionary aspects of 11 with the practicality of 4. Spiritual development for those with Master Number 22 involves learning to bring spiritual visions into the physical world. This might mean using your spiritual insights to create something tangible, whether it's a community project, a work of art, or a business that serves a higher purpose. For instance, you might feel called to start a socially responsible business or engage in work that contributes to societal well-being.

A key aspect of spiritual growth for Master Number 22 is understanding the balance between spiritual ideals and material reality. While 22 has the potential to manifest great things, it's important to stay connected to the spiritual principles that guide your actions. This means not getting too caught up in material success and always remembering the higher purpose behind your work. Practices such as visualization, goal setting with intention, and regular reflection on your spiritual values can help you stay aligned with the higher vibration of 22.

Master Number 33 is known as the "Master Teacher" and is associated with compassion, healing, and selfless service. Spiritual development for those with this number involves embracing the role of a healer or guide, using your gifts to uplift and support others. This might involve formal teaching or healing roles, but it can also manifest in everyday interactions where you offer guidance, support, or simply a compassionate presence.

For those with Master Number 33, spiritual growth also involves learning the importance of self-care and boundaries. The high vibration of 33 can lead to a tendency to give too much of oneself, sometimes at the expense of personal well-being. Incorporating regular self-care practices and learning to say no when necessary are crucial for maintaining balance. Engaging in spiritual practices such as energy healing, prayer, or rituals that honor your own needs can help you stay aligned with the compassionate energy of 33 while ensuring that you do not deplete yourself.

Incorporating Master Numbers into your spiritual development is about recognizing the unique lessons and energies these numbers bring and using them to guide your growth. Whether through intuitive practices, manifesting spiritual ideals, or serving others with compassion, aligning with your Master Number can elevate your spiritual journey, helping you reach higher levels of consciousness and fulfillment.

CHAPTER 12: COMPATIBILITY AND RELATIONSHIPS IN NUMEROLOGY

Numerology and Relationship Compatibility

In numerology, relationship compatibility is understood through the lens of numbers, each representing specific energies, traits, and tendencies. By comparing the core numbers in your numerology chart with those of a partner, you can gain insights into how well your energies align, where potential conflicts might arise, and how you can navigate your relationship more harmoniously.

The key numbers to consider in relationship compatibility are the Life Path Number, Expression Number, and Soul Urge Number. Each of these numbers provides a different perspective on your personality, desires, and communication style, making them crucial for understanding how you and your partner interact.

Life Path Numbers are the most significant when assessing compatibility. They reveal the fundamental path and lessons each person is meant to follow in life. For example, if one partner has a Life Path Number 1, they are likely to be independent, ambitious, and driven by a desire to lead. If the other partner has a Life Path Number 2, they may be more cooperative, sensitive, and focused on partnership. While these traits can complement each other, the 1's need for independence might sometimes clash with the 2's desire for closeness and cooperation. Recognizing this dynamic helps both partners understand their differences and find a balance that works for them.

Another important number is the **Expression Number**, which reflects your natural talents and how you express yourself in the world. For instance, someone with an Expression Number 3 might be highly creative, sociable, and expressive, thriving in environments where they can share their ideas freely. If their partner has an Expression Number 4, they may be more practical, organized, and focused on structure. While the 3's spontaneity might energize the relationship, the 4's need for stability could sometimes feel restrictive to the 3. Understanding these tendencies allows each partner to appreciate the other's strengths and find ways to support each other's expression.

The **Soul Urge Number** reveals your deepest desires and what you need to feel fulfilled on an emotional and spiritual level. For example, a person with a Soul Urge Number 5 craves freedom, adventure, and variety. They might feel most alive when exploring new experiences or embracing change. If their partner has a Soul Urge Number 6, which is centered around family, responsibility, and harmony, they may prioritize stability and nurturing relationships. While these needs can complement each other, the 5's desire for adventure might sometimes conflict with the 6's need for security. By recognizing these differences, the couple can work together to meet each other's needs, balancing the 5's need for freedom with the 6's desire for stability.

Numerology can also help you understand the **challenges** and **growth opportunities** within your relationship. For example, if both partners have a Master Number, such as 11, 22, or 33, the relationship may carry intense spiritual energy and high expectations. Master Numbers bring a heightened sense of purpose, but they also come with challenges related to their high vibration. In a relationship, this can lead to a dynamic where both partners push each other to achieve great things, but it might also create pressure or tension if the energy is not balanced.

Compatibility in numerology is not about finding a perfect match but about understanding how your energies interact. Even if two people have numbers that seem incompatible, awareness of these differences can lead to greater understanding and cooperation. For example, a Life Path 8 (associated with power and material success) and a Life Path 7 (associated with introspection and spirituality) might initially seem at odds. However, by recognizing the strengths each brings to the relationship, the 8 can appreciate the 7's depth and wisdom, while the 7 can learn to value the 8's drive and determination.

Numerology provides a framework for understanding relationship dynamics and finding ways to work together more effectively. By exploring the core numbers in your chart and those of your partner, you can gain insights into your relationship, helping you navigate challenges and deepen your connection. Whether you're looking to strengthen an existing relationship or understand a new one, numerology offers a powerful tool for enhancing your understanding of each other and creating a more harmonious partnership.

Comparing Life Path Numbers for Relationship Insights

Life Path Numbers in numerology are essential for understanding the fundamental characteristics and life goals of each person in a relationship. By comparing Life Path Numbers, you can gain insights into how well your energies align, where potential conflicts may arise, and how you can navigate your relationship more harmoniously.

For example, if one partner has a **Life Path Number 1**, they are likely independent, ambitious, and driven by a desire to lead and achieve. This person might be focused on their personal goals and may value autonomy and initiative. If their partner has a **Life Path Number 2**, which is associated with cooperation, sensitivity, and diplomacy, they may prioritize partnership, emotional connection, and harmony. While these traits can complement each other—where the 1 leads and the 2 supports—there is also potential for tension. The 1's strong need for independence might clash with the 2's desire for closeness and collaboration, leading to misunderstandings or conflicts over priorities.

In another scenario, if both partners have a **Life Path Number 3**, which is linked to creativity, self-expression, and social interaction, the relationship might be lively, dynamic, and full of shared activities. However, with both partners seeking attention and validation, there could be competition or a lack of balance if one person feels overshadowed by the other. Understanding this dynamic allows both partners to make space for each other's creative expressions and to ensure that communication remains open and supportive.

A couple with a **Life Path Number 4** and a **Life Path Number 5** might experience contrasting needs, with the 4 valuing stability, order, and discipline, and the 5 craving freedom, adventure, and change. The 4 might feel frustrated by the 5's desire for variety and spontaneity, while the 5 could feel restricted by the 4's focus on structure and routine. Recognizing these differences helps both partners appreciate each other's strengths—where the 4 provides a solid foundation and the 5 introduces excitement and flexibility into the relationship.

Even when Life Path Numbers seem mismatched, such as a **Life Path 7** (introspective, spiritual) paired with a **Life Path 8** (ambitious, material-focused), understanding the underlying motivations of each number can lead to a deeper connection. The 7's quest for inner knowledge can balance the 8's drive for external success, creating a relationship where both spiritual and material needs are respected and fulfilled.

Comparing Life Path Numbers offers a roadmap for understanding each partner's inherent traits, life goals, and challenges. By recognizing how your numbers interact, you can better support each other's growth, navigate differences with empathy, and strengthen your bond. This awareness fosters a more harmonious relationship where both partners feel understood and valued for who they are.

The Role of Destiny and Soul Urge Numbers in Relationships

Destiny and Soul Urge Numbers in numerology play a significant role in shaping the dynamics of a relationship. These numbers reveal deeper aspects of each person's personality and desires, offering insights into how well partners align on a spiritual and emotional level.

The Destiny Number represents your life's purpose and the talents you are meant to develop and share with the world. In a relationship, comparing Destiny Numbers helps you understand each partner's broader goals and how these align or differ. For instance, if one partner has a Destiny Number 6, they are likely drawn to nurturing roles, focusing on family, community, and creating harmony. If the other partner has a Destiny Number 8, they may be more focused on achieving success, leadership, and financial security.

While these goals can complement each other—where the 6 provides emotional support and the 8 builds material stability—conflicts might arise if the 6 feels neglected in the pursuit of the 8's ambitions, or if the 8 feels constrained by the 6's emphasis on home and relationships. Understanding these dynamics allows both partners to appreciate each other's contributions and work together to balance their differing priorities.

The Soul Urge Number reveals your innermost desires and what you need to feel fulfilled on an emotional and spiritual level. This number is important in how you connect with your partner on a deeper, more intimate level. For example, if one partner has a Soul Urge Number 2, they deeply desire emotional connection, harmony, and partnership. If their partner has a Soul Urge Number 5, they may crave freedom, adventure, and variety. These differing needs can lead to tension if not addressed—where the 2 might feel insecure about the 5's need for independence, and the 5 might feel suffocated by the 2's desire for closeness.

However, by understanding each other's Soul Urge Numbers, partners can find ways to meet each other's needs without compromising their own. For instance, the 2 can learn to appreciate the 5's adventurous spirit, while the 5 can make a conscious effort to provide the emotional security that the 2 needs. This mutual understanding fosters a relationship where both partners feel emotionally satisfied and spiritually aligned.

In relationships where both partners have the same Destiny or Soul Urge Number, the connection can be very strong, but it can also present challenges. For example, two people with a Destiny Number 9 might both be driven by a desire to help others and make a difference in the world. While this shared purpose can create a deep bond, it might also lead to overextension if both partners prioritize their humanitarian goals over the relationship. Recognizing this potential pitfall allows the couple to create boundaries and ensure that their personal connection remains strong.

By exploring Destiny and Soul Urge Numbers, couples can gain a deeper understanding of each other's life goals and emotional needs. This awareness helps to create a more fulfilling and balanced relationship, where both partners can grow individually and together.

How Numerology Can Improve Communication and Harmony

Numerology can be a powerful tool for improving communication and harmony in relationships by offering insights into each partner's unique personality traits, desires, and challenges. Understanding the core numbers in your numerology chart—such as the Life Path, Expression, and Soul Urge Numbers—can help you and your partner navigate your differences, enhance your communication, and foster a more harmonious connection.

Life Path Numbers are particularly useful for understanding the fundamental approach each person takes in life. For example, someone with a Life Path Number 1 may be assertive, independent, and goal-oriented, often leading the way in decision-making. In contrast, a partner with a Life Path Number 9 might be more compassionate, idealistic, and focused on broader humanitarian goals. Recognizing these traits can help both partners appreciate each other's perspectives and find common ground in their approach to shared decisions.

Expression Numbers, which reflect how you express yourself and interact with the world, can also shed light on communication styles. For instance, a person with an Expression Number 3 might be naturally expressive, social, and enjoy lively discussions. If their partner has an Expression Number 4, they may be more reserved, practical, and prefer structured, logical conversations. Understanding these differences can help each partner adapt their communication style to better connect with the other. The 3 might learn to tone down their exuberance in serious discussions, while the 4 can work on being more open to creative or emotional expression.

Soul Urge Numbers reveal deep-seated desires and emotional needs, which are crucial for understanding what each partner requires to feel loved and fulfilled. For example, a partner with a Soul Urge Number 6 may crave a stable, nurturing environment and feel most fulfilled when their relationship is harmonious and secure. If their partner has a Soul Urge Number 7, they might need more space for introspection and solitude to feel balanced. Recognizing these needs can help prevent misunderstandings—where the 6 might otherwise perceive the 7's need for alone time as withdrawal, and the 7 might view the 6's desire for closeness as clinginess. By acknowledging and respecting each other's emotional needs, both partners can create a more harmonious and supportive relationship.

Numerology also helps in identifying and addressing potential conflicts. For example, if one partner's Life Path or Destiny Number suggests a focus on material success and ambition (like an 8), and the other's indicates a preference for spiritual growth and inner fulfillment (like a 7), conflicts may arise around lifestyle choices, priorities, or values. Understanding these differences allows both partners to discuss their needs openly and find compromises that respect both perspectives.

Additionally, numerology can be used to set relationship goals that align with both partners' strengths. If one partner's chart highlights strong leadership abilities and the other's emphasizes nurturing and support, they can consciously work together to create a balanced dynamic where both roles are honored. This can be particularly effective in resolving conflicts and ensuring that both partners feel valued and understood.

In essence, numerology offers a detailed map of each partner's traits, preferences, and challenges, which can be used to improve communication and harmony in the relationship. By applying this knowledge, couples can better navigate their differences, enhance their connection, and create a more balanced and fulfilling partnership.

CHAPTER 13: NUMEROLOGY IN CAREER AND FINANCES

Using Numerology to Choose a Career Path

Numerology can be a powerful framework for choosing a career path that aligns with your natural talents, personality, and life purpose. By understanding the numbers in your numerology chart, particularly your Life Path Number, Expression Number, and Destiny Number, you can gain insights into the types of careers that are most likely to bring you fulfillment and success.

The Life Path Number is one of the most significant indicators when considering your career. This number, derived from your birth date, represents the core of who you are and the path you are meant to follow in life. For example, if your Life Path Number is 1, you are naturally inclined toward leadership, independence, and innovation. Careers that allow you to take charge, such as entrepreneurship, management, or any field where you can pioneer new ideas, are likely to be fulfilling for you. You might thrive as a business owner, a CEO, or in a role where you can drive progress and be recognized for your achievements.

If your Life Path Number is 6, on the other hand, you are likely drawn to roles that involve care, responsibility, and service to others. You might find fulfillment in careers related to healthcare, education, counseling, or social work. The nurturing aspect of the number 6 aligns well with professions that require empathy, understanding, and a strong sense of duty. For example, you might excel as a nurse, teacher, therapist, or in any role where you can make a positive impact on others' lives.

The Expression Number, also known as the Destiny Number, reveals your natural talents and how you express yourself in the world. This number, derived from the letters of your full name, provides additional insights into the careers that suit you best. For example, if your Expression Number is 3, you are likely to be creative, communicative, and expressive. Careers in the arts, media, writing, or any field that allows you to use your communication skills creatively might be ideal for you. You might thrive as a writer, artist, actor, or public speaker, where you can share your ideas and inspire others.

If your Expression Number is 8, you are likely to have a strong sense of ambition, discipline, and a desire for material success. Careers in finance, law, real estate, or any field that involves management and organization might be well-suited to you. You might excel in roles that require strategic thinking, leadership, and a focus on achieving tangible results. For example, you could find success as a financial advisor, corporate executive, or lawyer, where your skills in handling complex situations and making important decisions can shine.

The Destiny Number provides a broader perspective on your life's purpose and how you can achieve it through your career. For example, if your Destiny Number is 9, you are likely drawn to humanitarian work, helping others on a global scale, or pursuing a career that involves giving back to society. Careers in non-profit organizations, international relations, or any field that allows you to work for the greater good may align with your life's mission. You might find fulfillment as a social worker, environmentalist, or human rights advocate, where you can contribute to causes that matter deeply to you.

Incorporating numerology into your career decision-making process involves not only understanding these core numbers but also reflecting on how they align with your passions, skills, and life experiences. For instance, if you have a Life Path Number that suggests leadership but your current experience lies in a creative field, you might consider roles that allow you to combine these strengths, such as leading a creative team or starting your own artistic venture.

Numerology can also guide you in making career changes or pursuing new opportunities. If you find that your current job doesn't align with your numerological insights, it might be time to explore other options that better match your natural talents and life purpose. By following the guidance of your numbers, you can choose a career path that not only brings you success but also aligns with your true self, leading to greater satisfaction and fulfillment in your professional life.

How Expression and Personality Numbers Influence Career Success

In numerology, the Expression Number and Personality Number play significant roles in shaping your career success. These numbers offer insights into your natural talents, how you express yourself, and how others perceive you—factors that are crucial in determining your professional path and how you navigate your career.

The Expression Number, also known as the Destiny Number, is derived from the full name given at birth. It reflects your innate abilities and the potential you have to achieve your life's purpose. For example, if your Expression Number is 5, you are likely to be versatile, adaptable, and thrive in dynamic environments. Careers that offer variety, freedom, and the opportunity to travel or engage in multiple activities are well-suited to you. You might excel in roles such as marketing, public relations, sales, or journalism, where you can use your communication skills and adaptability to thrive in fast-paced settings.

On the other hand, if your Expression Number is 7, you might be more inclined toward analytical, research-oriented, or spiritual careers. You may find success in roles that require deep thinking, such as a scientist, philosopher, psychologist, or researcher. Your ability to focus, analyze, and seek deeper understanding can lead you to excel in fields where attention to detail and a quest for knowledge are paramount.

The Personality Number, derived from the consonants in your full name, reveals how others perceive you and how you present yourself to the world. This number can significantly influence your career success by shaping first impressions and how you interact with colleagues, clients, and superiors. For instance, if your Personality Number is 3, you are likely perceived as charismatic, creative, and socially engaging. This charm can be a valuable asset in careers that involve networking, public speaking, or any role that requires a strong public presence. Your ability to connect with others easily can open doors and create opportunities that might not be as accessible to someone with a less outwardly engaging personality.

If your Personality Number is 8, you might be seen as authoritative, ambitious, and business-minded. Others may naturally look to you for leadership or expect you to take charge in professional settings. This perception can be advantageous in careers that require strong organizational skills and the ability to make decisive decisions, such as in finance, law, or management. Your authoritative presence can help you climb the corporate ladder, earn respect from peers, and lead teams effectively.

Together, the Expression and Personality Numbers provide a comprehensive view of how you can leverage your natural talents and how you are perceived by others to achieve career success. By understanding and aligning with these numbers, you can choose roles that maximize your strengths and navigate professional relationships more effectively. For example, if you have a creative Expression Number but a more reserved Personality Number, you might thrive in roles where you can express your creativity in a controlled, behind-the-scenes manner, such as in writing or design.

Ultimately, these numbers guide you toward career paths that align with your true self, helping you achieve success and fulfillment in your professional life.

The Role of Personal Year Numbers in Financial Planning

Personal Year Numbers in numerology provide a blueprint for the themes and energies that will influence you over the course of a year. Understanding your Personal Year Number can be particularly useful in financial planning, as it offers insights into the best times for saving, investing, taking risks, or consolidating your financial position.

To calculate your Personal Year Number, add the digits of your birth day and month to the digits of the current year. For example, if your birthday is April 15 and you're calculating for the year 2024, you add 4 + 15 + 2024 (4 + 1 + 5 + 2 + 0 + 2 + 4 = 18, and 1 + 8 = 9). So, your Personal Year Number for 2024 would be 9.

Personal Year 1 marks the beginning of a new nine-year cycle, making it an ideal time for new financial ventures. This is a year for setting the stage for future growth. You might consider starting a new business, making significant investments, or pursuing new income streams. Financial decisions made during a Personal Year 1 often set the tone for the entire cycle, so it's important to be bold yet strategic.

Personal Year 4 is a time for building and consolidating. Financially, this year is best spent on saving, budgeting, and ensuring that your financial foundation is strong. It's a good year for paying off debts, investing in long-term assets like real estate, or improving your financial literacy. The energy of Year 4 encourages discipline and practicality, making it less about taking risks and more about securing your future.

Personal Year 5 brings change, freedom, and unpredictability. This year might involve unexpected expenses or financial opportunities. Flexibility is key, so it's wise to have a financial cushion and be open to adjusting your plans. While this year can be financially rewarding, it also carries the risk of impulsive decisions. Consider any major financial moves carefully, balancing your desire for freedom with a need for stability.

Personal Year 8 is a particularly powerful year for finances. This year is about power, success, and material gain. It's an excellent time for advancing your career, seeking promotions, or making strategic investments. The energy of Year 8 supports financial growth and the manifestation of wealth, so it's a year to be ambitious and focused on your financial goals. However, it's also important to manage resources wisely and avoid becoming overly materialistic.

Each Personal Year Number brings its own set of opportunities and challenges for financial planning. By aligning your financial strategies with the energies of your Personal Year, you can make more informed decisions, optimize your financial growth, and navigate potential pitfalls more effectively.

Numerology for Wealth and Abundance

Numerology offers insight into how you can attract wealth and abundance into your life by aligning your actions with the energies of your core numbers. By understanding your Life Path, Expression, and Personal Year Numbers, you can create a roadmap for financial success and abundance.

Life Path Numbers provide the foundation for your approach to wealth. For example, if your Life Path Number is 8, you are naturally inclined toward financial success and leadership. The number 8 is associated with power, ambition, and material wealth. To harness the energy of 8, focus on building a strong work ethic, taking calculated risks, and pursuing leadership roles that can lead to financial gain.

You might thrive in careers related to finance, business, or any field that allows you to manage resources and make strategic decisions.

For a Life Path Number 3, attracting wealth might involve leveraging creativity and communication skills. The number 3 is associated with self-expression, creativity, and social interaction. Careers in the arts, entertainment, or media might be particularly lucrative for you. To attract abundance, focus on networking, sharing your ideas, and exploring creative ventures that can bring financial rewards.

Expression Numbers reveal the talents and abilities that can lead to financial success. If your Expression Number is 4, you are likely to excel in roles that require organization, discipline, and attention to detail. The number 4 is associated with building strong foundations, so focusing on careers that involve project management, engineering, or any field that requires a methodical approach can lead to long-term financial stability. Your path to wealth might involve slow and steady growth, building your finances through consistent effort and careful planning.

If your Expression Number is 6, wealth might come through nurturing and service-oriented roles. The number 6 is linked to responsibility, care, and harmony. You might find financial success in careers related to healthcare, counseling, or education, where your ability to care for others is rewarded. To attract abundance, focus on creating value for others and building relationships that lead to financial opportunities.

Personal Year Numbers also play a role in your financial journey. For instance, during a Personal Year 1, it's a good time to start new ventures or make significant financial decisions that set the stage for future growth. In a Personal Year 8, the focus is on achieving financial goals, manifesting wealth, and advancing in your career.

To attract wealth and abundance using numerology, it's essential to align your actions with the energies of your numbers. This might involve pursuing careers that resonate with your Life Path or Expression Numbers, setting financial goals that align with your Personal Year Number, or using your unique talents to create value in ways that lead to financial rewards.

By understanding and applying the principles of numerology, you can tap into the energies that support wealth and abundance, creating a life of financial success that is aligned with your true self.

CHAPTER 14: NUMEROLOGY AND HEALTH

Understanding the Connection Between Numbers and Health

In numerology, each number carries specific vibrations that influence various aspects of life, including health. Understanding the connection between numbers and health can provide insights into your physical and mental well-being, guiding you toward a more balanced and healthy lifestyle.

Life Path Numbers are central in numerology and play a significant role in shaping your health tendencies. Each Life Path Number is associated with particular traits and challenges that can impact your physical and emotional health. For example, if you have a Life Path Number 1, you are likely to be highly driven, ambitious, and independent. While these traits can lead to success, they can also create stress and tension, which might manifest as headaches, high blood pressure, or issues related to the heart. It's essential for someone with a Life Path Number 1 to incorporate regular relaxation techniques, such as meditation or yoga, to manage stress effectively and maintain heart health.

In contrast, a Life Path Number 6 is associated with nurturing, responsibility, and a strong focus on family and community. While these qualities can create a harmonious environment, they can also lead to overextending oneself, resulting in fatigue or stress-related ailments like digestive issues or back pain. People with this Life Path need to prioritize self-care and ensure they are not neglecting their own health needs while caring for others.

Expression Numbers, which reflect your natural talents and how you express yourself, also influence your health. For instance, an Expression Number 3 is associated with creativity, communication, and social interaction. Individuals with this number may thrive in social settings and enjoy activities that allow them to express themselves, but they might also be prone to anxiety or throat-related issues if they feel misunderstood or unable to communicate effectively. Ensuring that they have healthy outlets for self-expression, such as art or writing, can help maintain their mental and physical health.

If your **Expression Number** is 8, you might be driven by a desire for power, success, and financial stability. While these traits can lead to great achievements, they can also create a tendency to overwork and neglect personal well-being. People with an Expression Number 8 might experience stress-related conditions such as insomnia, digestive problems, or issues with joints and bones. It's crucial for them to balance their ambitious nature with adequate rest, a healthy diet, and regular physical activity to prevent burnout and maintain overall health.

Personal Year Numbers also play a role in your health, as they reflect the energies influencing you during a specific year. For example, during a Personal Year 4, the focus is on building stability and structure. This year might encourage you to establish healthier routines and focus on long-term health goals, such as adopting a balanced diet, starting a regular exercise regimen, or addressing chronic health issues. However, the disciplined energy of Year 4 can also lead to rigidity or overwork, so it's essential to incorporate flexibility and relaxation into your health routines.

In a **Personal Year 5**, which is associated with change, freedom, and unpredictability, you might feel more inclined to explore new health practices or make significant lifestyle changes. This could be a good time to try new fitness activities, experiment with different diets, or take a more adventurous approach to your well-being. However, the energy of Year 5 can also lead to impulsive decisions or inconsistency, so it's important to stay grounded and avoid extreme or risky health choices.

Understanding the connection between numerology and health involves recognizing how the vibrations of your core numbers influence your physical and mental well-being. By aligning your lifestyle with the energies of your numbers, you can make more informed health decisions, address potential weaknesses, and enhance your overall vitality. For instance, if you know that your Life Path Number suggests a tendency toward stress, you can proactively incorporate stress management techniques into your daily routine. Similarly, understanding the challenges of your Expression and Personal Year Numbers allows you to create a balanced approach to health that supports your long-term well-being.

Numerology offers a unique perspective on health, emphasizing the importance of balance and alignment with your natural energies. By paying attention to the guidance of your numbers, you can create a healthier, more harmonious life, ensuring that both your body and mind are well cared for.

How Life Path and Soul Urge Numbers Affect Well-Being

In numerology, both Life Path and Soul Urge Numbers offer insights into your overall well-being. These numbers, derived from your birth date and full name, respectively, influence not only your personality and life choices but also your physical and emotional health.

Life Path Numbers reveal the core of who you are and the path you are meant to follow in life. Each Life Path Number is associated with specific traits that can significantly impact your health. For example, if your Life Path Number is 3, you are likely to be naturally creative, expressive, and social. These traits are wonderful for fostering a vibrant, active lifestyle, but they can also lead to issues like anxiety or stress if you feel creatively stifled or socially isolated. People with a Life Path 3 should focus on activities that allow them to express themselves, such as art, writing, or public speaking, to maintain their emotional well-being.

If your Life Path Number is 7, you might be more introspective, analytical, and spiritually inclined. While these qualities can lead to a rich inner life, they might also result in a tendency toward isolation or overthinking, which could manifest as mental fatigue or even depression. To support their well-being, individuals with a Life Path 7 should ensure they balance their introspective tendencies with social interaction and physical activity, which can help ground their energy and prevent them from becoming too withdrawn.

Soul Urge Numbers, on the other hand, represent your innermost desires and what you need to feel fulfilled on a deeper level. These numbers are important in your emotional health. For instance, if your Soul Urge Number is 2, you likely have a deep need for harmony, relationships, and emotional connection. When these needs are met, you thrive; however, if you experience conflict or feel emotionally disconnected, it can lead to stress, anxiety, or even heart-related issues. To maintain well-being, those with a Soul Urge 2 should prioritize relationships that bring peace and avoid environments that are overly chaotic or confrontational.

For someone with a Soul Urge Number 9, the drive to help others and engage in humanitarian efforts is strong. This altruistic nature can be incredibly fulfilling, but it can also lead to burnout if the individual neglects their own needs in the process of caring for others. People with a Soul Urge 9 should ensure they balance their desire to serve with self-care practices, such as regular relaxation and setting boundaries to prevent emotional exhaustion.

Understanding the influence of your Life Path and Soul Urge Numbers on your well-being allows you to make choices that support your physical and emotional health. By aligning your lifestyle with the natural tendencies of these numbers, you can create a more harmonious and fulfilling life.

Identifying Health Challenges Through Numerology

Numerology offers a unique perspective on identifying potential health challenges by examining the core numbers in your numerology chart. Each number carries specific vibrations that influence not only your personality and life path but also your physical and emotional health. By understanding the energies associated with your Life Path, Expression, and Personal Year Numbers, you can gain insights into areas of your health that may require attention.

Life Path Numbers are a fundamental aspect of numerology and can provide clues about your general health tendencies. For example, individuals with a Life

Path Number 4 are typically hardworking, disciplined, and focused on building stability in their lives. However, these traits can sometimes lead to health challenges related to stress, rigidity, and overwork. People with this Life Path Number might be prone to issues like back problems, joint stiffness, or digestive disorders, especially if they neglect to balance their work with relaxation and self-care. Regular physical activity and stress management techniques are essential for maintaining their well-being.

If you have a Life Path Number 5, you are likely adventurous, freedom-loving, and drawn to change. While these traits can lead to an exciting and dynamic life, they can also result in health challenges if not managed properly. Individuals with a Life Path 5 might be prone to accidents, nervous system issues, or problems related to overindulgence, such as addiction. It's important for those with this number to find healthy outlets for their energy and to establish routines that support their health, such as regular exercise and a balanced diet.

Expression Numbers reveal how you express yourself and interact with the world, which can also highlight potential health challenges. For example, if your Expression Number is 6, you may have a strong sense of responsibility and a deep desire to care for others. While these traits are admirable, they can lead to burnout or stress-related illnesses if you neglect your own needs. Individuals with an Expression Number 6 should be mindful of setting boundaries and ensuring they take time for self-care to prevent exhaustion and maintain their health.

Personal Year Numbers indicate the energies and themes that will influence you during a specific year. Understanding your Personal Year Number can help you anticipate health challenges that may arise during that time. For instance, a Personal Year 7 is often a time of introspection, spiritual growth, and learning. While this year can be mentally stimulating, it can also lead to health issues related to overthinking, anxiety, or feeling isolated. During a Personal Year 7, it's important to balance introspective activities with social interaction and physical exercise to support your mental and emotional health.

By examining these numerological aspects, you can identify potential health challenges and take proactive steps to address them. This awareness allows you to tailor your lifestyle to better align with your numbers, promoting a healthier, more balanced life.

Using Numerology for Preventive Health Strategies

Numerology can be a powerful tool for developing preventive health strategies tailored to your unique energy patterns. By understanding the influences of your core numbers, such as your Life Path, Expression, and Personal Year Numbers, you can create a proactive approach to health that helps prevent potential issues before they arise.

Life Path Numbers provide a broad overview of your inherent tendencies, including how you approach your health. For example, if you have a Life Path Number 2, you are likely sensitive, peace-loving, and attuned to the emotions of others. While these qualities are strengths, they can also make you prone to stress-related health issues, such as anxiety or digestive problems, particularly if you internalize others' emotions or experience conflict. A preventive strategy for someone with a Life Path 2 might include regular mindfulness practices, meditation, and activities that promote inner peace, such as yoga or tai chi. These practices help maintain emotional balance and prevent stress from impacting your physical health.

For individuals with a Life Path Number 8, who are often driven, ambitious, and focused on material success, health challenges might arise from overwork and a tendency to neglect self-care. Preventive strategies for a Life Path 8 could include setting regular work-life boundaries, incorporating stress-relief practices like exercise or hobbies into daily routines, and ensuring adequate rest to prevent burnout. Maintaining a balanced diet and staying hydrated are also essential for supporting the high energy levels required by this Life Path.

Expression Numbers highlight your natural talents and how you express yourself, which can also inform your approach to preventive health. If your Expression Number is 3, you are likely creative, social, and communicative. However, you might also be prone to throat-related issues or stress if you feel creatively stifled or misunderstood. Preventive health strategies for an Expression Number 3 might include engaging in regular creative activities, such as writing, art, or music, to ensure you have healthy outlets for self-expression. Additionally, practicing good vocal health, such as staying hydrated and avoiding overuse of your voice, can help prevent related health issues.

Personal Year Numbers reflect the specific energies and challenges that will influence you during a particular year, guiding your health focus for that period. For instance, during a Personal Year 9, which is often associated with completion, reflection, and letting go, it's an ideal time to focus on cleansing and detoxifying your body and mind. This might involve adopting a healthier diet, incorporating detox practices like fasting or juicing, and engaging in activities that help release emotional or mental clutter, such as journaling or therapy.

By understanding the energies of your numerological chart, you can develop preventive health strategies that align with your natural tendencies and the specific challenges you may face. This proactive approach helps you maintain balance, avoid potential health issues, and enhance your overall well-being. Whether it's through stress management, creative expression, or periodic detoxification, numerology offers insights into how you can best care for your body and mind throughout your life.

CHAPTER 15: ADVANCED NUMEROLOGY TECHNIQUES

Introduction to Name Numerology

Name numerology is a core aspect of numerology that explores the significance of your name in shaping your personality, destiny, and life path. In name numerology, each letter of your name corresponds to a specific number, and these numbers combine to reveal deeper insights into who you are and the energies that influence your life. Understanding name numerology can offer powerful guidance in both personal growth and making important life decisions.

At the heart of name numerology are several key numbers: the Expression Number, the Personality Number, and the Soul Urge Number. Each of these numbers provides a different perspective on your character and the forces that shape your experiences.

The Expression Number, also known as the Destiny Number, is derived from the full name you were given at birth. This number represents your natural talents, abilities, and the overall potential you have in life. It reflects what you are meant to accomplish and the skills you are likely to develop. To calculate your Expression Number, assign each letter in your full name a corresponding number based on its position in the alphabet (A=1, B=2, C=3, etc.), then add these numbers together. If the sum is a double-digit number, reduce it by adding the digits together until you reach a single digit (unless the result is a Master Number like 11, 22, or 33, which are not reduced).

For example, if your name is "John Smith," you would calculate the numbers for each letter as follows:

- J = 1
- O = 6
- H = 8
- N = 5
- S = 1
- M = 4
- I = 9
- T = 2
- H = 8

Adding these together: 1 + 6 + 8 + 5 + 1 + 4 + 9 + 2 + 8 = 44. Then, 4 + 4 = 8. So, the Expression Number for "John Smith" is 8. This number indicates a person with strong leadership qualities, a drive for success, and a natural ability to manage resources and people. Understanding your Expression Number helps you align with your life's purpose and make choices that leverage your innate strengths.

The Personality Number is calculated using the consonants in your full name. This number reveals how others perceive you, essentially the face you show to the world. It reflects your outward personality, your first impression on others, and the image you project. To find your Personality Number, follow the same process as with the Expression Number, but only include the consonants. This number gives you insights into how you are likely to be received by others and how you can adjust your outward behavior to better align with your goals.

For instance, if "John Smith" calculates his Personality Number using only the consonants (J, H, N, S, M, T, H), the calculation would be:

- J = 1
- H = 8
- N = 5
- S = 1
- M = 4
- T = 2
- H = 8

Adding these together: 1 + 8 + 5 + 1 + 4 + 2 + 8 = 29, and then 2 + 9 = 11. Since 11 is a Master Number, it is not reduced further. A Personality Number of 11 indicates someone who is seen as intuitive, inspiring, and possibly a leader with a strong spiritual presence.

The Soul Urge Number, or Heart's Desire Number, is derived from the vowels in your full name. This number reveals your innermost desires, what you truly want out of life, and what motivates you at a deep level. It's a reflection of your true self and the driving force behind your actions. To calculate your Soul Urge Number, use the same method but focus only on the vowels in your name.

Using "John Smith" as an example, the vowels are O and I:

- O = 6
- I = 9

Adding these together: 6 + 9 = 15, and 1 + 5 = 6. The Soul Urge Number here is 6, indicating a deep desire to care for others, create harmony, and be involved in nurturing roles, whether in family, community, or work settings. Knowing your Soul Urge Number can help you understand what truly fulfills you and guide you toward pursuits that align with your heart's desires.

Name numerology is more than just a series of calculations; it's a tool for self-discovery and personal empowerment. By understanding the numbers associated with your name, you gain insights into your strengths, challenges, and the path you are meant to follow. These numbers provide a blueprint for navigating life, helping you make decisions that are in harmony with your true self. Whether you're considering a career change, navigating relationships, or seeking personal growth, name numerology offers a deeper understanding of the energies that shape your life and how you can work with them to achieve your goals.

By incorporating the wisdom of name numerology into your life, you can enhance your self-awareness, improve your interactions with others, and move more confidently toward your aspirations.

The Power of Changing Your Name

In numerology, your name carries a unique vibrational energy that influences your life path, personality, and destiny. Changing your name can significantly alter these vibrations, potentially transforming your experiences and the way you interact with the world. The power of changing your name lies in the ability to align your personal energy with your aspirations, enhance certain traits, or mitigate challenges indicated by your original name.

When you change your name, you are essentially altering the numbers that define your Expression, Personality, and Soul Urge Numbers. Each letter in your name corresponds to a specific number, and these numbers combine to form the vibrational blueprint that influences your life. For example, if you feel that your current name doesn't fully support your life goals or personal growth, changing it can create a new numerical profile that aligns better with your desired path.

Expression Number is one of the most significant aspects influenced by a name change. This number reflects your natural talents, abilities, and potential. If you were born with an Expression Number that suggests challenges or limitations in certain areas, changing your name can shift these energies. For instance, if your original Expression Number is 4, which is associated with discipline, structure, and hard work but may feel limiting if you're seeking more creativity or freedom, changing your name might result in an Expression Number that better aligns with your aspirations, such as a 3 or 5, which are more closely linked to creativity, communication, and adaptability.

Changing your name can also affect your **Personality Number**, which influences how others perceive you. If you've struggled with being misunderstood or if you feel that the impression you give doesn't reflect who you truly are, altering your name can help you project a different image. For example, if your original Personality Number is 7, which can make you appear reserved, introspective, or aloof, and you want to be seen as more approachable and sociable, you might choose a name that changes your Personality Number to 3, which is associated with charisma and social ease.

The **Soul Urge Number** is another critical aspect influenced by a name change. This number reveals your innermost desires and what truly drives you. If your current name's Soul Urge Number doesn't resonate with your deepest aspirations, changing your name can help align your inner motivations with your external reality. For example, if your original Soul Urge Number is 8, which focuses on power, success, and material wealth, but you seek a more compassionate, nurturing life, you might change your name to result in a Soul Urge Number of 6, which is more aligned with care, responsibility, and service to others.

It's important to note that changing your name doesn't erase the influence of your birth name entirely. The original vibrational energies will still play a role in your life, especially in the areas of your life linked to your foundational identity, such as family and early childhood experiences. However, by consciously choosing a new name, you can introduce new energies that help you grow in the directions you desire.

Many people experience profound changes after altering their names. Celebrities, business people, and spiritual seekers often change their names to enhance their public image, attract success, or align more closely with their spiritual path. For example, someone pursuing a career in the arts might choose a stage name that gives them an Expression Number associated with creativity and public recognition, such as 3 or 9.

However, the decision to change your name should not be taken lightly. It's essential to carefully consider the new name's numerical impact on your life. Consulting with a numerologist can provide insights into how different names will influence your vibrational energy and help you choose a name that aligns with your goals.

In short, changing your name can be a powerful tool for personal transformation in numerology. By altering the numerical vibrations associated with your name, you can realign your energy with your aspirations, enhance your natural talents, and project the image you desire. Whether you seek greater success, better relationships, or deeper fulfillment, a name change can open new doors and guide you toward the life you envision.

Addressing Complex Numerology Charts

In numerology, most people are familiar with basic concepts like Life Path, Expression, and Soul Urge Numbers. However, some numerology charts are more complex, with overlapping influences, Master Numbers, Karmic Debt Numbers, and conflicting energies that can make interpretation challenging. Addressing these complexities requires a deeper understanding of numerological principles and an ability to synthesize multiple factors into a coherent narrative.

One of the first steps in addressing a complex numerology chart is identifying **Master Numbers**. Master Numbers, such as 11, 22, and 33, are powerful and carry higher vibrations than their single-digit counterparts. They often indicate potential for greater spiritual growth, leadership, or creative achievement. However, Master Numbers also bring challenges, such as heightened sensitivity or pressure to live up to high expectations. In a complex chart, multiple Master Numbers can create tension or conflicting energies. For instance, someone with both an 11 and a 22 might struggle between the intense spiritual insight of the 11 and the practical, material-focused ambitions of the 22. Balancing these energies involves acknowledging both aspects and finding ways to integrate them, such as pursuing a career that combines spiritual and practical elements.

Karmic Debt Numbers add another layer of complexity. These numbers, such as 13, 14, 16, and 19, suggest that the individual is carrying unresolved issues from past lives or earlier in this life that must be addressed in the present. If a chart has multiple Karmic Debt Numbers, it indicates that the individual is likely to face significant challenges that require careful navigation. For example, a person with a Life Path Number 4 (derived from 13) and a Destiny Number 14 may need to work through issues related to discipline, stability, and freedom. The presence of these numbers requires a focus on balancing the karmic lessons while also pursuing personal goals. Addressing Karmic Debt involves acknowledging the past patterns and making conscious efforts to overcome them, such as by developing better discipline or learning to manage freedom responsibly.

Conflicting energies within a chart can also create complexity. For example, a person with a Life Path Number 7, which is introspective and spiritual, combined with an Expression Number 8, which is ambitious and material-focused, may feel torn between these two aspects of their identity. Navigating this conflict requires a nuanced approach, such as finding ways to incorporate both spirituality and ambition into their life. This might involve pursuing a career that allows for introspection and personal growth while also providing opportunities for leadership and success.

Another challenge in complex numerology charts is the presence of **overlapping influences**. For example, if multiple numbers in the chart indicate similar traits, such as a focus on creativity or communication, this can create a strong emphasis in one area of life. While this might be beneficial, it can also lead to an imbalance if other aspects of life are neglected. Addressing this requires a holistic view of the chart, ensuring that all areas of life are considered and balanced. For instance, if creativity is strongly indicated, but there is little emphasis on stability or relationships, the individual might need to consciously focus on building these aspects to create a more balanced life.

When interpreting complex charts, it's also important to consider **transit cycles and pinnacles**, which are longer-term influences that can shift the focus of life over time. Understanding how these cycles interact with the core numbers in the chart can provide insights into the timing of challenges or opportunities. For instance, a person entering a Pinnacle Number 9 cycle might experience a period of endings and completions, which could be challenging if their core numbers are focused on building and growth. Recognizing these cycles allows for better planning and preparation, helping the individual navigate transitions more smoothly.

In summary, addressing complex numerology charts requires a deep understanding of how different numbers interact and influence each other. By carefully analyzing Master Numbers, Karmic Debt Numbers, conflicting energies, and overlapping influences, you can create a comprehensive and balanced interpretation of the chart. This approach allows you to guide individuals through their challenges, helping them leverage their strengths, address their weaknesses, and achieve greater harmony in their lives.

Exploring the Numerology of Addresses and Locations

In numerology, the energy of an address or location can significantly influence the experiences of those who live or work there. Just as your name and birthdate carry specific vibrational energies, so do the numbers associated with your home, office, or any other important place. Understanding the numerology of addresses can help you choose locations that align with your goals, promote harmony, and enhance your overall well-being.

To explore the numerology of an address, you first need to reduce the numbers in the address to a single digit, as you would with other numerology calculations. For example, if you live at 123 Main Street, you would add the numbers together: $1 + 2 + 3 = 6$. Therefore, the address has the vibration of the number 6. Each number, from 1 to 9, as well as the Master Numbers 11 and 22, carries its own unique energy that influences the environment.

Number 1 addresses are associated with independence, leadership, and new beginnings. Living or working in a number 1 location is ideal for people who are self-starters, entrepreneurs, or those seeking to establish their identity. The energy of 1 promotes innovation and personal growth but can also feel isolating if not balanced with social connections.

Number 2 addresses foster partnerships, cooperation, and harmony. These locations are well-suited for couples, families, or businesses that rely on teamwork. The energy of 2 is nurturing and supportive, creating a peaceful atmosphere. However, it's essential to maintain balance, as too much of the 2 energy can lead to over-dependence or difficulty making decisions.

Number 3 addresses are vibrant, creative, and social. These locations are ideal for artists, entertainers, or anyone who thrives on communication and expression. The energy of 3 promotes joy and optimism, making it a great place for hosting gatherings or pursuing creative projects. On the flip side, it can also lead to scattered energy if not managed properly.

Number 4 addresses are grounded, stable, and practical. These locations are perfect for those who value structure, discipline, and hard work. The energy of 4 supports long-term planning and building a solid foundation. However, it can feel rigid or restrictive if not balanced with flexibility and spontaneity.

Number 5 addresses are dynamic, adventurous, and full of change. These locations are ideal for people who love variety, travel, and excitement. The energy of 5 encourages freedom and exploration but can also lead to restlessness or instability if not grounded by other energies.

Number 6 addresses are nurturing, loving, and family-oriented. These locations are perfect for families, caregivers, or anyone focused on creating a harmonious home. The energy of 6 promotes responsibility and service to others, making it an excellent place for fostering close relationships. However, it's essential to avoid overburdening oneself with too many responsibilities.

Number 7 addresses are introspective, spiritual, and peaceful. These locations are ideal for those who seek solitude, meditation, or spiritual growth. The energy of 7 encourages reflection and inner wisdom but can feel isolating if not balanced with social interaction.

Number 8 addresses are powerful, ambitious, and focused on material success. These locations are perfect for entrepreneurs, business people, or anyone driven to achieve financial goals. The energy of 8 promotes authority and leadership but can also lead to stress or workaholism if not balanced with relaxation and enjoyment.

Number 9 addresses are compassionate, humanitarian, and globally oriented. These locations are ideal for those who want to make a positive impact on the world, whether through philanthropy, teaching, or spiritual work. The energy of 9 supports altruism and generosity but can also lead to feelings of sacrifice or loss if not balanced with self-care.

Master Number 11 addresses carry a high vibration of intuition, inspiration, and spiritual insight. These locations are ideal for healers, visionaries, or anyone pursuing a spiritual path. The energy of 11 encourages enlightenment and creativity but can also lead to nervous tension if not grounded.

Master Number 22 addresses are powerful and capable of turning dreams into reality. These locations are perfect for those who want to build something lasting and impactful, whether it's a business, a community, or a legacy. The energy of 22 supports large-scale projects and practical achievements but requires careful planning to avoid becoming overwhelmed.

When choosing a location, it's important to consider how the energy of the address aligns with your personal goals and lifestyle. For example, if you're starting a new business, a number 1 or 8 address might support your ambitions. If you're looking for a peaceful retreat, a number 7 or 2 address might be more suitable. Understanding the numerology of addresses can help you create environments that support your aspirations and enhance your quality of life.

Numerology and Business Naming

In numerology, the name of your business carries a specific vibrational energy that can influence its success, reputation, and overall impact. Choosing the right business name is more than just a matter of branding; it's about aligning your business's energy with your goals and values. Numerology can guide you in selecting a name that resonates with prosperity, growth, and the specific qualities you want your business to embody.

To analyze the numerology of a business name, you start by assigning each letter in the name a corresponding number, just as you would with a person's name. For example, the name "Acme Consulting" would be analyzed by converting the letters to numbers (A=1, C=3, M=4, E=5, etc.) and then adding those numbers together. If the sum is a double-digit number, it is usually reduced to a single digit, unless it's a Master Number like 11, 22, or 33, which are not reduced.

Number 1 business names carry the energy of leadership, innovation, and independence. A business with a number 1 name is likely to stand out in its field, driven by ambition and a pioneering spirit. This type of business is well-suited for entrepreneurs who are starting something new or breaking into a competitive market. For example, "Pioneer Technologies" might sum to a number 1, indicating a business that leads the way in its industry.

Number 2 business names are associated with partnerships, cooperation, and diplomacy. These businesses often thrive on collaboration and customer relationships. A number 2 name is ideal for businesses that focus on services, such as counseling, mediation, or consulting. An example might be "Harmony Consulting," which could add up to a number 2, suggesting a business built on creating balance and fostering positive relationships.

Number 3 business names resonate with creativity, communication, and entertainment. These businesses are likely to attract attention and engage customers through their innovative ideas and vibrant energy. A number 3 name is perfect for businesses in the arts, media, or marketing. For instance, "Creative Spark Media" might total a number 3, indicating a business that excels in expressive and imaginative ventures.

Number 4 business names embody stability, structure, and reliability. These businesses are grounded and methodical, often associated with industries that require precision and attention to detail. A number 4 name is well-suited for businesses in construction, engineering, or finance. "Foundation Builders" could be an example, suggesting a business that is solid, dependable, and focused on long-term growth.

Number 5 business names are dynamic, adaptable, and adventurous. These businesses thrive on change and innovation, making them ideal for industries that are fast-paced or constantly evolving. A number 5 name might be chosen for a travel agency, technology startup, or entertainment company. "Dynamic Ventures" could add up to a number 5, reflecting a business that embraces new opportunities and thrives on excitement.

Number 6 business names are nurturing, responsible, and community-oriented. These businesses often focus on service, care, and creating a harmonious environment. A number 6 name is ideal for businesses in healthcare, education, or hospitality. An example might be "Care & Comfort Homes," suggesting a business dedicated to providing a nurturing and supportive atmosphere.

Number 7 business names are associated with introspection, spirituality, and research. These businesses are often involved in fields that require deep thinking, analysis, or spiritual guidance. A number 7 name is well-suited for businesses in academia, wellness, or consulting. "Insight Solutions" might be an example, indicating a business that provides thoughtful and profound insights.

Number 8 business names carry the energy of power, success, and material wealth. These businesses are driven to achieve financial success and authority in their industry. A number 8 name is perfect for businesses in finance, real estate, or executive leadership. "Wealth Management Group" could sum to a number 8, reflecting a business that focuses on generating prosperity and influence.

Number 9 business names are linked to compassion, humanitarian efforts, and global awareness. These businesses often focus on making a positive impact on the world, whether through philanthropy, education, or environmental sustainability. A number 9 name might be chosen for a non-profit organization or a socially responsible business. "Global Outreach Foundation" could be an example, indicating a business dedicated to serving humanity and making a difference.

Master Numbers in business names, such as 11, 22, or 33, carry higher vibrations and indicate potential for significant impact. A business with a Master Number name might be seen as a leader in its field, with the ability to inspire, build, or heal on a large scale. For example, a business named "Visionary Enterprises" with a Master Number 11 might be driven by innovative ideas and spiritual insight, aiming to bring enlightenment to its industry.

Choosing a business name in alignment with numerology ensures that the vibrational energy of the name supports your business's mission, values, and goals. By selecting a name that resonates with your desired energy, you can attract the right customers, build a strong reputation, and ultimately achieve success. Numerology can help you find a business name that aligns with your vision and fosters prosperity.

CHAPTER 16: PRACTICAL APPLICATIONS OF NUMEROLOGY

Numerology for Daily Decision Making

Numerology is not just about understanding your life path or personality traits; it can also be a practical tool for making daily decisions. By tapping into the vibrational energy of numbers, you can gain insights into the best times to act, how to approach specific situations, and what to expect from your interactions. Incorporating numerology into your daily routine can help you navigate life more smoothly, making decisions that align with your personal energy and the universe's rhythms.

One of the simplest ways to use numerology in daily decision-making is through **Personal Day Numbers**. Your Personal Day Number is calculated by adding the day's date to your Life Path Number. This number gives you a sense of the day's energy and how it aligns with your own. For example, if today is the 15th of the month, and your Life Path Number is 4, you would add $1 + 5 + 4 = 10$, and then reduce it to $1 + 0 = 1$. So, your Personal Day Number is 1. A Personal Day 1 is ideal for new beginnings, making decisions, and taking initiative. It's a day to start new projects, assert yourself, and set the tone for future success.

If your Personal Day Number is 2, the energy of the day is more about cooperation, relationships, and patience. It's a good day for meetings, negotiations, or resolving conflicts. You might find that working in partnership or focusing on diplomacy yields better results than going it alone. For instance, if you're planning a discussion with a colleague, a Personal Day 2 might be the perfect time to approach them with a collaborative mindset, ensuring that both parties feel heard and understood.

Personal Month Numbers work similarly but give you a broader view of the energy influencing your decisions over an entire month. To calculate your Personal Month Number, add the month's number to your Life Path Number. For example, if it's August (the 8th month) and your Life Path Number is 3, you would add $8 + 3 = 11$, which is a Master Number and isn't reduced. A Personal Month 11 is a time of heightened intuition, spiritual growth, and inspiration. It's a period to trust your gut feelings and focus on creative or spiritual pursuits.

On the other hand, a Personal Month 4 is about discipline, structure, and hard work. It's a time to focus on organization, planning, and building solid foundations. If you're deciding when to tackle a major project or reorganize your life, a Personal Month 4 would be the ideal time to do so. This period encourages you to put in the necessary effort to ensure long-term stability.

Numerology can also guide your financial decisions. By understanding the energy of specific numbers, you can choose the best days for financial activities like investing, signing contracts, or making significant purchases. For example, a Personal Day 8 is often associated with power, success, and material gain, making it an ideal day for business dealings, financial negotiations, or making important career decisions. If you're considering a significant investment, choosing a day with the energy of 8 can align your actions with the vibrations of wealth and authority.

If you're planning a purchase, particularly something that involves beauty, harmony, or aesthetics, a Personal Day 6 might be more suitable. The energy of 6 is associated with love, balance, and responsibility, making it a good day for decisions related to home, family, or anything that requires a nurturing touch. For instance, if you're redecorating your home or buying a gift for a loved one, a day with the energy of 6 will likely result in a choice that brings harmony and satisfaction.

Relationships and communication can also benefit from numerology. Understanding the numerology of a particular day can help you choose the best times to have important conversations, resolve conflicts, or deepen connections. For example, a Personal Day 3 is associated with creativity, joy, and communication. It's an excellent day for socializing, expressing your thoughts, or engaging in creative collaborations. If you're planning to give a presentation, share ideas, or connect with friends, a day with the energy of 3 can enhance your communication and ensure your message is well-received.

Conversely, a Personal Day 7 is more introspective and spiritual, making it a better time for reflection, meditation, or solo work. It's not the best day for social activities or starting new projects, but it's perfect for gaining insight, studying, or connecting with your inner self. If you're faced with a decision that requires deep thought or spiritual consideration, choosing a day with the energy of 7 can help you access the wisdom you need.

Planning trips or important events can also be influenced by numerology. For example, if you're planning a vacation, you might want to choose dates that align with the energy of 5, which is associated with freedom, adventure, and change. A Personal Month or Day with the energy of 5 can enhance your travel experience, bringing excitement and new opportunities. On the other hand, if you're planning a more restful, home-centered activity, the energy of 6 or 2 might be more appropriate, providing a sense of peace and comfort.

Incorporating numerology into your daily decision-making doesn't require extensive calculations or complex rituals. It's about understanding the energy of the numbers that influence your life and using that knowledge to make choices that align with your goals and well-being. By tuning into the vibrational energy of the days, months, and your personal numbers, you can navigate life with greater confidence and clarity, making decisions that support your growth, happiness, and success.

Using Numerology for Personal and Spiritual Growth

By understanding the energies associated with your personal numbers—such as your Life Path Number, Expression Number, and Soul Urge Number—you can align your actions with your true self, fostering growth in all areas of your life.

Life Path Numbers provide the foundation for personal growth in numerology. This number, derived from your birthdate, reveals the broad lessons and themes you will encounter throughout your life. For example, if your Life Path Number is 7, your spiritual growth might center around introspection, wisdom, and seeking deeper truths. You may find fulfillment in practices like meditation, study, and spiritual exploration. Understanding your Life Path Number allows you to recognize the unique path you're on and encourages you to embrace the lessons it presents, whether they involve developing patience, resilience, or inner peace.

If your Life Path Number is 9, your growth may involve themes of compassion, humanitarian efforts, and global consciousness. This number often calls for you to serve others and make a positive impact on the world. By aligning your actions with these themes—perhaps through volunteering, mentoring, or supporting charitable causes—you can experience profound personal fulfillment and spiritual growth.

Expression Numbers, which reflect your natural talents and abilities, also have a key role in personal growth. Knowing your Expression Number helps you understand the gifts you are meant to develop and share with the world. For instance, if your Expression Number is 3, your growth might involve nurturing your creative talents, whether through writing, art, or public speaking. Embracing these abilities allows you to express your true self and find joy in your endeavors.

Conversely, if your Expression Number is 8, your personal growth may focus on developing leadership skills, financial acumen, and the ability to manage resources effectively. By honing these talents, you can achieve significant success and make a lasting impact in your chosen field. Recognizing the strengths associated with your Expression Number helps you set meaningful goals and take actions that lead to both personal satisfaction and professional achievement.

Soul Urge Numbers reveal your deepest desires and what you truly need to feel fulfilled. This number reflects your inner motivations and guides your spiritual growth. If your Soul Urge Number is 6, your growth might involve cultivating a loving, nurturing environment, whether within your family, community, or workplace. By focusing on relationships and creating harmony, you align with your soul's deepest needs, leading to a more satisfying and balanced life.

For those with a Soul Urge Number 11, spiritual growth is often centered around intuition, enlightenment, and inspiring others. You may be drawn to roles that involve teaching, healing, or guiding others on their spiritual journeys. Embracing these roles and trusting your intuition can lead to profound personal growth and a deeper connection with your higher self.

Numerology also offers insights into the **challenges and obstacles** you may encounter, which are essential for growth. Karmic Debt Numbers, for example, indicate areas where you may need to address past actions or unresolved issues. Understanding these challenges helps you approach them with mindfulness and intention, turning obstacles into opportunities for growth.

Finally, **Personal Year Numbers** guide you through the specific themes and energies of each year in your life. By aligning your actions with the energy of your Personal Year, you can maximize your growth and make the most of the opportunities that arise. For example, a Personal Year 1 is ideal for new beginnings and setting the stage for future growth, while a Personal Year 9 encourages reflection, completion, and letting go of what no longer serves you.

Incorporating numerology into your personal and spiritual growth journey allows you to gain a deeper understanding of yourself and your life's purpose. By aligning with the energies of your core numbers, you can navigate your path with greater clarity, make decisions that support your growth, and ultimately, live a more fulfilling and spiritually enriched life.

How to Interpret Recurring Numbers in Your Life

Recurring numbers in your life are not mere coincidences; they are often messages from the universe, guiding you toward greater awareness and understanding. In numerology, these repeated patterns carry significant meaning, offering insights into your current life circumstances, spiritual path, or decisions you need to make. Interpreting recurring numbers requires paying attention to the context in which they appear and understanding their vibrational energy.

One of the most common recurring numbers people notice is **11:11**. This number is often seen as a spiritual wake-up call, indicating that you are aligned with your higher purpose or that a new spiritual journey is beginning. When you repeatedly see 11:11, it's a signal to pay attention to your thoughts and intentions, as they are likely manifesting rapidly. This number encourages you to focus on your true desires and align your actions with your spiritual path.

Another frequent occurrence is the repetition of **Master Numbers**, such as 22 or 33. Master Number 22, for example, is known as the "Master Builder," representing the ability to turn dreams into reality. If you frequently encounter the number 22, it may suggest that you have the power to manifest your goals through hard work, discipline, and vision. It's a reminder to stay focused on your long-term objectives and to build something lasting and meaningful.

Similarly, Master Number 33, often associated with the "Master Teacher," carries the vibration of compassion, guidance, and selfless service. If you see 33 repeatedly, it may be a call to step into a role where you can help others, whether through teaching, healing, or leading by example. This number encourages you to use your gifts for the benefit of others and to pursue paths that promote collective well-being.

Recurring single-digit numbers also carry specific meanings. For example, seeing the number **4** repeatedly might indicate a need for structure, stability, and grounding. The energy of 4 is associated with building strong foundations, so its recurrence could be a message to focus on organizing your life, establishing routines, or addressing practical matters that need attention. If you're in the midst of chaos or uncertainty, the repeated appearance of 4 may be urging you to create more order and discipline in your life.

The number **7**, on the other hand, is often linked to spirituality, introspection, and wisdom. If you frequently encounter the number 7, it may be a sign that you need to take time for reflection, study, or connecting with your inner self. This number often appears when you are being called to deepen your spiritual practice or when you need to trust your intuition in making decisions. The repetition of 7 can be a reminder to seek knowledge, embrace solitude, and focus on your spiritual journey.

When interpreting recurring numbers, it's essential to consider the **context** in which they appear. For example, if you keep seeing the number 5 during a period of significant change, it might be a sign that you are on the right path and that these changes are leading to greater freedom and growth. The number 5 is associated with adventure, adaptability, and transformation, so its recurrence during times of transition can be a reassuring message that you are moving in the right direction.

Recurring numbers can also serve as **personal reminders**. For instance, if the number 9 keeps appearing, it might be a prompt to let go of something that no longer serves you, as 9 is the number of completion, endings, and humanitarianism. It could be urging you to release old patterns, relationships, or habits that are hindering your progress and to focus on serving others or pursuing a higher purpose.

To fully interpret recurring numbers, it's helpful to keep a journal and note the times and circumstances in which they appear. Over time, patterns may emerge that provide deeper insights into their meanings. Pay attention to your thoughts, feelings, and surroundings when these numbers appear, as they often provide clues to the messages being conveyed.

In short, recurring numbers are powerful symbols in numerology, offering guidance and insights into your life's journey. By paying attention to these patterns and understanding their vibrational meanings, you can gain valuable direction, make informed decisions, and align more closely with your spiritual and personal growth.

Combining Numerology with Other Metaphysical Practices

Numerology's effectiveness can be enhanced when combined with other metaphysical practices. By integrating numerology with practices such as astrology, tarot, or crystal healing, you can gain deeper insights into your life and enhance your spiritual growth. Each of these practices brings its own unique energy and perspective, and when used together, they create a more holistic approach to understanding yourself and the world around you.

Astrology is one of the most natural complements to numerology. Both systems are based on the idea that the universe operates according to specific energies and patterns that can be deciphered. While numerology focuses on the vibrational energy of numbers, astrology is concerned with the influence of celestial bodies on your personality, behavior, and life events. By combining these two practices, you can gain a more detailed and nuanced understanding of yourself.

For example, if your Life Path Number is 5, which is associated with freedom, change, and adventure, you might look at your astrological chart to see where these traits are emphasized. If you have strong placements in Sagittarius, a sign known for its love of exploration and new experiences, this would reinforce the energy of your Life Path Number. Conversely, if your chart is dominated by a more grounded and stable sign like Taurus, you might need to work on balancing these conflicting energies. By understanding both your numerological and astrological profiles, you can navigate your life with greater clarity and make decisions that align with your true nature.

Tarot is another metaphysical practice that pairs well with numerology. Each tarot card is associated with a specific number, and understanding these numerological connections can deepen your readings. For instance, the tarot's Major Arcana cards are numbered from 0 (The Fool) to 21 (The World), and each number carries its own significance. If you draw The Magician (card number 1) during a reading, and your Life Path Number is also 1, this could indicate that the reading is particularly relevant to your sense of self and the new beginnings or opportunities you are about to encounter.

You can also use numerology to guide your tarot practice. For example, if you're entering a Personal Year 7, a year focused on introspection and spiritual growth, you might choose to work with tarot cards that align with this energy, such as The Hermit (card number 9), which represents solitude and inner wisdom. This intentional alignment helps you focus on the themes most relevant to your current life phase, enhancing the clarity and depth of your tarot readings.

Crystal healing is another practice that can be effectively combined with numerology. Each crystal has its own vibrational frequency, which can be matched to the energy of specific numbers. For example, if you're working with the energy of the number 6, which is associated with love, harmony, and responsibility, you might choose to work with rose quartz, a crystal known for its heart-healing properties. If you're focusing on the energy of the number 8, which is linked to power, success, and abundance, citrine or pyrite could be more appropriate choices, as these stones are often used to attract wealth and prosperity.

By combining numerology with crystal healing, you can create more personalized and targeted energy practices. For instance, if your Expression Number is 3, and you're seeking to enhance your communication skills, you might meditate with a blue lace agate, a crystal known to support clear expression and throat chakra activation. Pairing your numerological insights with specific crystals allows you to work more effectively with your energy, fostering growth and healing in a focused and intentional way.

Meditation and affirmations can also be enhanced through the integration of numerology. By using your core numbers, you can create personalized affirmations that resonate with your unique energy. For instance, if your Soul Urge Number is 2, which is connected to harmony and relationships, your affirmations might focus on attracting peaceful connections and fostering balance in your interactions. Meditating on your Life Path or Expression Number while reciting these affirmations can help you align more closely with your true self and your life purpose.

Combining numerology with other metaphysical practices allows you to tap into multiple layers of insight and energy, creating a richer, more comprehensive spiritual practice. Whether you're looking to understand your life path, enhance your intuitive abilities, or attract specific energies into your life, integrating numerology with astrology, tarot, crystal healing, and other practices can provide the guidance and support you need to grow and thrive on your spiritual journey.

Developing Your Own Numerology Practice

Developing your own numerology practice is a deeply personal and empowering journey. It allows you to connect with the vibrational energies of numbers, understand their influence on your life, and use this knowledge to make informed decisions, set goals, and navigate challenges. Whether you're just starting or looking to deepen your practice, there are several steps you can take to create a numerology routine that is meaningful and effective.

Start with the basics by learning how to calculate your core numbers, such as your Life Path Number, Expression Number, Soul Urge Number, and Personality Number. These numbers form the foundation of your numerology practice, offering insights into your personality, life purpose, and the challenges you may face. To calculate your Life Path Number, for example, you add the digits of your birth date until you arrive at a single digit (unless it's a Master Number like 11, 22, or 33). Understanding the meanings and energies associated with these numbers is crucial for interpreting your numerology chart and applying it to your life.

As you become more comfortable with these calculations, **explore deeper aspects** of numerology, such as Karmic Debt Numbers, Personal Year Numbers, and Pinnacle Numbers. These elements add layers of complexity to your practice, offering more detailed insights into your life's journey. For instance, Karmic Debt Numbers indicate unresolved issues from past lives or earlier in this life that need to be addressed. Understanding these numbers helps you recognize patterns in your life and take conscious steps to resolve them, leading to personal growth and transformation.

Create a daily or weekly numerology routine to stay connected with the energies influencing your life. One effective practice is to calculate your Personal Day or Personal Month Numbers and reflect on how they align with your current experiences. For example, if your Personal Day Number is 9, you might focus on completing tasks, letting go of what no longer serves you, or helping others. Keeping a numerology journal where you note these numbers and reflect on their impact can help you track patterns and gain a deeper understanding of how numerology influences your daily life.

Incorporate numerology into your goal-setting process by aligning your objectives with the energies of your core numbers. For instance, if your Expression Number is 4, which is associated with discipline and structure, you might set goals that focus on building a solid foundation in your career, finances, or personal life. By understanding the strengths and challenges associated with your numbers, you can set realistic goals that align with your natural tendencies and increase your chances of success.

Use numerology as a tool for reflection and self-awareness. Regularly reviewing your numerology chart can help you stay in tune with your life's purpose and identify areas where you may need to focus your attention. For example, if you notice that your Karmic Debt Number is influencing your current challenges, you can take proactive steps to address these issues, such as seeking guidance, practicing forgiveness, or making changes in your behavior. This reflective practice helps you stay aligned with your spiritual growth and personal development.

Expand your practice by integrating other metaphysical tools that resonate with you. As mentioned earlier, combining numerology with practices like astrology, tarot, or crystal healing can enhance your understanding and application of numerology. For example, you might use tarot cards to explore the themes suggested by your Personal Year Number or meditate with crystals that align with your Life Path Number. These complementary practices add depth and richness to your numerology practice, allowing you to explore your spiritual journey from multiple angles.

Teach others about numerology as you gain confidence in your practice. Sharing your knowledge with friends, family, or through online platforms can deepen your understanding and help you connect with a community of like-minded individuals. Teaching also reinforces your learning and can lead to new insights as you explain concepts to others. Whether you're offering personal readings, writing about numerology, or simply discussing it with those close to you, teaching is a powerful way to solidify your practice and continue your growth.

Finally, **trust your intuition** as you develop your numerology practice. While learning the technical aspects of numerology is important, it's equally crucial to listen to your inner guidance. Numerology is as much an art as it is a science, and your intuition can often lead you to deeper insights and understanding. Allow yourself to experiment, explore, and find the methods that resonate most with you.

Developing your own numerology practice is an ongoing journey of self-discovery and spiritual growth. By learning the foundational elements, creating a regular routine, and integrating other metaphysical practices, you can build a numerology practice that is uniquely tailored to your needs and goals. This practice will not only enhance your understanding of yourself but also empower you to navigate life with greater clarity, purpose, and confidence.

CHAPTER 17: HISTORICAL TIMELINE OF NUMEROLOGY

Timeline of Numerology

4000 BCE – The Earliest Roots in Mesopotamia
The origins of numerology can be traced back to ancient Mesopotamia, where early civilizations began associating numbers with mystical and spiritual significance. The Sumerians, who thrived in the region that is now modern-day Iraq, are known to have developed one of the earliest number systems. Their base-60 system, which is still used today to measure time and angles, was not just practical but also held spiritual meaning. Numbers like 3, 7, and 12 were considered sacred and were often used in religious rituals and astronomical calculations. This era marks the beginning of numbers being seen as more than mere tools for counting—they were imbued with divine attributes.

3000 BCE – The Numerology of Ancient Egypt
By 3000 BCE, the Egyptians had also begun to explore the mystical significance of numbers. Egyptian priests and scholars associated numbers with gods and cosmic principles. For example, the number 2 was often linked to duality, such as the balance between life and death, while the number 3 represented the concept of completeness, which can be seen in their understanding of the triad of gods like Osiris, Isis, and Horus. Numbers were integral to Egyptian architecture, as seen in the precise measurements of the pyramids, which were designed with specific numerical proportions believed to align with cosmic forces.

2000 BCE – The Influence of the Babylonians
The Babylonians, who succeeded the Sumerians in Mesopotamia, further developed the idea of numbers having a mystical connection with the cosmos. They were skilled astronomers and mathematicians, and their contributions to numerology are evident in their use of numbers in astrology. The Babylonians believed that the movements of celestial bodies could be understood and predicted through numerical patterns. They developed the zodiac, a system still in use today, which relies heavily on the numerological significance of planetary movements.

1500 BCE – The Vedic Numerology of Ancient India
Around 1500 BCE, in ancient India, the earliest texts of the Vedas were composed. These texts contain references to the significance of numbers in understanding the universe and the self. Vedic numerology, which is one of the oldest known systems, was based on the belief that each number from 1 to 9 corresponds to certain planets and energies. The number 3, for example, is linked to Jupiter and is associated with wisdom and expansion. Vedic scholars used these numerical associations to interpret a person's life path and destiny, laying the groundwork for what would later evolve into more structured numerological systems in India.

1000 BCE – Pythagoras and the Mystical Power of Numbers
Though Pythagoras himself lived later, by 1000 BCE, the Greek fascination with numbers had already begun to take shape. The Greeks were deeply influenced by earlier Egyptian and Babylonian thought. They believed that numbers were the fundamental elements of reality. Pythagoras, often considered the father of numerology, would later expand on these ideas, teaching that numbers are not just quantities but also qualities with profound spiritual significance. The Pythagorean school would eventually develop the concept of the numerical vibration of names and dates, which is central to modern numerology.

600 BCE – Pythagoras and the Pythagorean School
Pythagoras, a Greek mathematician and mystic, founded a school in Croton (modern-day southern Italy) around 600 BCE. His teachings integrated mathematics, philosophy, and spirituality, and he famously declared that "All is number." Pythagoras and his followers believed that the universe was structured according to a mathematical order, and they explored the mystical properties of numbers, particularly the numbers 1 through 10. The Pythagorean theorem, still taught in schools today, was part of a broader belief that numbers have inherent properties that influence the physical and spiritual world. Pythagoras' work laid the foundations for Western numerology, particularly the idea that numbers correspond to specific qualities or vibrations.

500 BCE – The Numerology of the I Ching in China
In China, around 500 BCE, the I Ching (Book of Changes) was compiled, a text that is both a philosophical work and a manual of divination. The I Ching uses a system of 64 hexagrams, each made up of six lines that are either broken (yin) or unbroken (yang). These hexagrams are generated through numerical methods, such as casting yarrow sticks or coins, and each corresponds to a specific set of symbols and meanings. The I Ching reflects the deep Chinese belief in the interconnectedness of numbers, nature, and the cosmos, and it has influenced both Eastern and Western numerology.

300 BCE – Hellenistic Influence and the Spread of Numerology
By 300 BCE, the ideas of Pythagoras and his followers had spread throughout the Hellenistic world, influencing not only Greek but also Roman thought. Numerology began to merge with other mystical traditions, such as astrology and alchemy, as scholars sought to understand the divine order of the universe. This period saw the development of Gematria, a system that assigns numerical value to letters of the alphabet, which would later become an essential aspect of Kabbalistic numerology.

0 BCE – The Integration of Numerology into Religious and Philosophical Systems
As the Common Era approached, numerology was increasingly integrated into religious and philosophical systems across different cultures. In Jewish mysticism, the Kabbalah began to incorporate Gematria, using the numerical values of

Hebrew letters to find hidden meanings in sacred texts. Meanwhile, in the Roman Empire, numerology continued to be practiced alongside astrology and other divinatory arts, influencing early Christian thought as well. The idea that numbers have a mystical power that can reveal hidden truths about the universe and human destiny was now firmly established, setting the stage for the further development of numerology in the centuries to come.

0 – 100 CE – Early Christian Numerology and Biblical Interpretations

In the first century CE, early Christian scholars began to explore the symbolic meaning of numbers within the context of their faith. This period saw the development of biblical numerology, where numbers mentioned in the Bible were interpreted as carrying spiritual significance. For example, the number 3, symbolizing the Holy Trinity (Father, Son, and Holy Spirit), was seen as a number of divine perfection and completeness. The number 7, which appears frequently in the Bible, was understood as a symbol of spiritual perfection, often associated with creation and divine order. Early Christian numerology laid the groundwork for later mystical interpretations of the Bible, where numbers were seen as keys to understanding the divine mysteries hidden within the scriptures.

100 – 500 CE – The Rise of Gnosticism and Mystical Numerology

During the first few centuries of the Common Era, Gnosticism emerged as a significant religious and philosophical movement. Gnostics believed in the existence of hidden knowledge (gnosis) that could lead to spiritual enlightenment and salvation. Numerology played a vital role in Gnostic teachings, where numbers were used to decode spiritual truths and unlock deeper understandings of the universe. Gnostic texts often contain complex numerical symbolism, where numbers are used to represent spiritual beings, levels of reality, or stages of the soul's journey toward enlightenment. For example, the number 12 was often associated with the 12 aeons, or divine emanations, in the Gnostic cosmology. This period saw the blending of numerology with mystical and esoteric traditions, influencing both religious thought and occult practices.

200 – 300 CE – The Development of Kabbalistic Numerology

In the Jewish mystical tradition, known as Kabbalah, the practice of Gematria began to take on greater significance during the second and third centuries CE. Gematria is a system where each letter of the Hebrew alphabet is assigned a numerical value, and words or phrases are analyzed based on the sum of these values. Kabbalists used Gematria to uncover hidden meanings in the Torah and other sacred texts, believing that numbers could reveal divine truths and connect the physical world with the spiritual realms. For example, the Hebrew word for "life," chai (חי), has a numerical value of 18, making the number 18 a symbol of life and vitality in Jewish culture. The development of Kabbalistic numerology during this period laid the foundation for more elaborate numerical interpretations in later centuries.

300 – 500 CE – The Influence of Neoplatonism and Pythagorean Revival

Neoplatonism, a philosophical system that emerged in the third century CE, deeply influenced the intellectual and mystical traditions of the time. Neoplatonists, such as Plotinus and Proclus, drew heavily on the ideas of Plato and Pythagoras, emphasizing the importance of numbers in understanding the structure of the cosmos. For Neoplatonists, numbers were not just abstract concepts but living realities that reflected the underlying order of the universe. The number 1, representing the One or the Good, was seen as the source of all existence, while other numbers symbolized various levels of reality emanating from the One. This period saw a revival of Pythagorean numerology, where numbers were considered sacred symbols that could lead the soul to higher knowledge and union with the divine.

500 – 700 CE – The Spread of Numerology in the Islamic World

As the Islamic Empire expanded in the 7th century, numerological concepts began to spread throughout the Muslim world, influencing Islamic mysticism and philosophy. Islamic scholars and mystics, known as Sufis, integrated numerology into their spiritual practices, using numbers to understand the divine order and the nature of reality. One significant contribution was the development of the Abjad system, a form of Gematria in which Arabic letters were assigned numerical values. Sufis used the Abjad system to interpret the Quran and other sacred texts, believing that numerical patterns could reveal hidden spiritual meanings. For example, the number 99, representing the 99 names of Allah, was considered particularly sacred. The integration of numerology into Islamic thought during this period contributed to the broader development of esoteric and mystical traditions in the Islamic world.

700 – 800 CE – The Influence of Indian Numerology on Islamic Scholars

During the early Islamic Golden Age, there was significant cross-cultural exchange between the Islamic world and India. Islamic scholars encountered Indian numerology, particularly the Vedic numerological system, which associated numbers with planets and cosmic energies. Indian numerology had a profound influence on the development of Islamic numerology, particularly in the areas of astrology and mystical interpretations of numbers. Scholars such as Al-Kindi and Al-Farabi incorporated Indian numerical concepts into their works, blending them with Islamic and Greek philosophical traditions. This period saw the further refinement of numerological practices in the Islamic world, as scholars sought to understand the connections between numbers, the cosmos, and the divine.

800 – 1000 CE – The Integration of Numerology into Medieval Thought

By the 9th and 10th centuries, numerology had become an integral part of medieval intellectual and spiritual life in both the Islamic world and Europe. In the Islamic world, scholars such as Al-Kindi and Al-Farabi continued to explore the mystical significance of numbers, while in Europe, the works of earlier philosophers like Pythagoras and Plato were rediscovered and studied by scholars such as Boethius. These scholars believed that numbers were the key to understanding the structure of the universe and the mind of God. Numerology was used in a variety of contexts, from astrology and alchemy to architecture and music, reflecting the belief that numbers were the foundation of all creation. The integration of numerology into medieval thought laid the groundwork for the continued development of numerical mysticism in the Middle Ages and the Renaissance.

(This period, spanning from 0 to 1000 CE, marks the deepening of numerology as a mystical and philosophical practice, influencing religious thought, philosophy, and science across multiple cultures. As numerological concepts continued to evolve and spread, they laid the foundation for the rich traditions of numerology that would develop in the following centuries.)

1000 – 1100 CE – The Influence of Islamic Scholars and the Translation Movement

During the 11th century, the Islamic Golden Age continued to flourish, with scholars translating and preserving ancient Greek, Indian, and Persian texts on numerology, mathematics, and philosophy. This period saw significant contributions from scholars like Al-Ghazali, who integrated numerological concepts into Islamic theology and mysticism. The Abjad system, a form of numerology that assigns numerical values to Arabic letters, was used extensively in the interpretation of the Quran and in Sufi mystical practices. The Islamic scholars' work laid the foundation for the transmission of numerological knowledge to Europe through Spain and Sicily, where these texts would later be translated into Latin.

1100 – 1200 CE – The Emergence of Kabbalistic Numerology in Europe

The 12th century marked a pivotal moment in the development of numerology in Europe, particularly within Jewish mysticism. Kabbalistic numerology, which had been evolving for centuries, became more formalized during this period. Kabbalists in medieval Spain and Provence, such as Abraham Abulafia, developed complex systems of Gematria, where Hebrew letters were assigned numerical values to uncover hidden meanings in sacred texts. These mystical interpretations were not only used to deepen understanding of the Torah but also to explore the nature of God and the universe. The Kabbalistic Tree of Life, with its ten sefirot (emanations), is a key example of how numbers were used to represent different aspects of divine reality. This period solidified the importance of numerology within Kabbalistic thought and influenced Christian mystics who would later adopt similar practices.

1200 – 1300 CE – Numerology in Christian Mysticism and Scholasticism

By the 13th century, numerology began to play a more prominent role in Christian mysticism and scholastic thought. Influenced by the earlier works of Pythagoras, Plato, and Augustine, Christian scholars like Thomas Aquinas and Albertus Magnus explored the symbolic significance of numbers in the Bible and nature. The number 3, representing the Holy Trinity, and the number 7, symbolizing spiritual perfection, were frequently discussed in theological works. Additionally, the translation of Arabic texts into Latin introduced European scholars to Islamic numerology and mathematics, further enriching the numerological traditions in Christian Europe. During this time, numerology was seen as a way to understand the divine order of the universe and to uncover the hidden meanings in sacred texts and natural phenomena.

1300 – 1400 CE – The Renaissance of Numerology and the Influence of Hermeticism

The 14th century marked the beginning of the Renaissance, a period of renewed interest in classical knowledge, including numerology. The rediscovery of ancient Greek and Roman texts, along with the influence of Hermeticism, led to a revival of Pythagorean and Platonic numerology. Hermeticism, a spiritual and philosophical tradition based on the writings attributed to Hermes Trismegistus, emphasized the interconnectedness of all things and the belief that numbers were fundamental to understanding the cosmos. Renaissance scholars like Marsilio Ficino and Giovanni Pico della Mirandola were deeply influenced by these ideas, and they integrated numerology into their studies of philosophy, theology, and the arts. This period saw the development of numerological theories that linked the structure of the universe to mathematical and mystical principles, influencing everything from art and architecture to music and literature.

1400 – 1500 CE – The Rise of Occult Numerology and the Influence of Johannes Reuchlin

By the 15th century, numerology had become deeply entwined with the occult, as scholars and mystics sought to understand the hidden forces that governed the universe. One of the most significant figures of this period was Johannes Reuchlin, a German humanist and scholar who played a key role in introducing Kabbalistic numerology to Christian Europe. Reuchlin's work, particularly his book *De Arte Cabalistica* (On the Art of Kabbalah), bridged the gap between Jewish mysticism and Christian thought, arguing that Kabbalistic numerology could provide deeper insights into Christian theology. His work influenced many Renaissance thinkers, including Pico della Mirandola and Cornelius Agrippa, who would go on to write extensively about the mystical properties of numbers.

During this time, the invention of the printing press in the mid-15th century also facilitated the spread of numerological ideas. Texts on numerology, astrology, and the occult became more widely available, allowing these ideas to reach a broader audience. The period also saw the rise of numerology in the context of alchemy, where numbers were used to represent different stages of the alchemical process and the transformation of matter into spirit.

(This period from 1000 CE to 1500 CE was marked by a deepening of numerological thought, with influences from Islamic, Jewish, and Christian traditions blending to create a rich mixture of mystical and philosophical interpretations. Numerology became a key component of the intellectual and spiritual life of the Middle Ages and the Renaissance, influencing everything from theology to art and laying the groundwork for the further development of numerological practices in the modern era.)

1500 – 1600 CE – The Flourishing of Renaissance Numerology and Hermeticism

The 16th century was a period of intense intellectual and spiritual exploration, and numerology played a significant role in the Renaissance's broader cultural movement. Influenced by the rediscovery of ancient Greek, Roman, and Egyptian texts, scholars sought to integrate numerology into their understanding of the universe. The works of Marsilio Ficino, Giovanni Pico della Mirandola, and Johannes Reuchlin continued to influence thinkers, blending numerological ideas with Hermeticism, Kabbalah, and Christian mysticism.

The concept of the "Great Chain of Being," a hierarchical structure that connected all forms of life, from the divine to the mundane, was linked to numerology. Scholars believed that numbers were the key to understanding this divine order. For example, the number 4, representing stability and the four elements (earth, water, air, fire), was seen as foundational to the structure of the universe. Alchemists, who sought to transform base metals into gold and achieve spiritual enlightenment, also relied on numerology to guide their experiments, believing that numbers held the secrets to unlocking the mysteries of matter and spirit.

1600 – 1700 CE – The Influence of Alchemy, Astrology, and the Occult

The 17th century saw the continued blending of numerology with alchemy, astrology, and other occult practices. Figures like Robert Fludd, a prominent English physician and mystic, used numerology to explore the relationship between the microcosm (the individual) and the macrocosm (the universe). Fludd's work, particularly his *Utriusque Cosmi Historia* (History of the Two Worlds), emphasized the importance of numbers in understanding the divine order and the connection between humanity and the cosmos.

In addition to alchemy and astrology, numerology also played a role in the early development of modern science. Isaac Newton, known for his contributions to physics and mathematics, was also deeply interested in alchemy and numerology. Newton believed that numbers were not just abstract concepts but had real, divine significance that could reveal the secrets of the natural world. His work, while primarily scientific, was influenced by the belief that the universe was structured according to mathematical and numerological principles.

1700 – 1800 CE – The Enlightenment and the Decline of Numerology

The 18th century, known as the Age of Enlightenment, marked a shift towards reason, science, and skepticism. As rationalism and empiricism became the dominant intellectual currents, interest in numerology and other mystical practices began to decline. The Enlightenment emphasized observable facts and scientific inquiry over metaphysical speculation, leading to a distancing from numerological traditions that were seen as unscientific or superstitious.

However, numerology did not disappear entirely. It persisted in more esoteric circles, where it was practiced alongside other forms of occultism. Freemasonry, which gained prominence during this period, incorporated numerology into its rituals and symbolism. Numbers like 3, 7, and 33 held special significance in Masonic teachings, representing principles of divine harmony, spiritual perfection, and enlightenment. Despite the broader cultural shift away from mysticism, numerology continued to influence secret societies and individuals who sought to explore the spiritual dimensions of life beyond the bounds of conventional religion and science.

1800 – 1850 CE – The Romantic Revival of Mysticism and Numerology

The early 19th century saw a revival of interest in mysticism, spurred by the Romantic movement, which reacted against the rationalism of the Enlightenment. Romantics emphasized emotion, imagination, and the spiritual aspects of life, leading to a renewed fascination with numerology, astrology, and other esoteric practices. Figures like William Blake, the English poet and artist, incorporated numerological symbolism into their work. Blake's poetry and paintings often explored the mystical significance of numbers, particularly in the context of spiritual visions and the structure of the divine cosmos.

In addition to the Romantics, the early 19th century saw the rise of spiritualism, a movement that sought to communicate with the spirits of the dead. Spiritualists often used numerology to interpret messages from the spirit world, believing that numbers could reveal the presence and intentions of spirits. This period also witnessed the publication of numerous books on numerology and related topics, reflecting a growing popular interest in the occult.

1850 – 1900 CE – The Emergence of Modern Numerology and the New Thought Movement

The second half of the 19th century marked the beginning of what is now considered modern numerology. This period saw the rise of the New Thought movement, which emphasized the power of the mind, positive thinking, and the idea that individuals could shape their own reality through thought and intention. Numerology became a key component of New Thought teachings, as it was believed that numbers could reveal one's life path, personality, and destiny, and that understanding these numbers could help individuals align their thoughts and actions with the universe's natural laws.

By the end of the 19th century, numerology had become more systematized, with specific methods and interpretations being widely taught and practiced. This period also saw the beginnings of theosophy, a spiritual movement that sought to integrate Eastern and Western esoteric traditions, including numerology. Theosophists like Helena Blavatsky explored the connections between numbers, consciousness, and the spiritual evolution of humanity, further solidifying numerology's place in modern metaphysical thought.

(This timeline from 1500 to 1900 illustrates the evolution of numerology from its Renaissance roots through its incorporation into modern spiritual practices. Despite periods of decline, numerology persisted and adapted, influencing a wide range of intellectual and spiritual movements, and laying the foundation for its continued relevance in the 20th century and beyond.)

1900 – 1920 CE – The Birth of Modern Numerology

The early 20th century marked a significant period in the development of modern numerology. L. Dow Balliett, who was active in the late 19th and early 20th centuries, laid much of the groundwork for what would become the modern numerological system. Her books, including *The Philosophy of Numbers* and *Number Vibration in Questions and Answers*, emphasized the spiritual significance of numbers and their influence on personal destiny. Balliett's work was characterized by the integration of numerology with the New Thought movement, which promoted the idea that positive thinking and spiritual understanding could shape one's reality.

Balliett's teachings were expanded by her student, Dr. Juno Jordan, who further developed the system of calculating Life Path Numbers, Destiny Numbers, and other core numbers that are still used in modern numerology today. Dr. Jordan's contributions helped to codify numerology into a more structured and accessible system, allowing it to reach a broader audience.

1920 – 1940 CE – The Influence of the Occult and Esoteric Movements

The 1920s and 1930s saw a resurgence of interest in the occult, including numerology, as people sought spiritual answers in the aftermath of World War I. This period was marked by the influence of theosophy, which integrated Eastern and Western spiritual traditions, and promoted the idea that numbers were key to understanding the spiritual dimensions of existence.

Paul Foster Case, a prominent American occultist and founder of the Builders of the Adytum (B.O.T.A.), was one of the key figures in promoting numerology during this time. Case incorporated numerology into his teachings on the Tarot and the Kabbalah, emphasizing the idea that numbers were not only symbolic but also powerful tools for spiritual transformation. His work helped to bridge the gap between numerology and other esoteric practices, making it a central component of Western occultism.

1940 – 1960 CE – Numerology in Popular Culture and Self-Help Movements

By the mid-20th century, numerology had begun to enter popular culture, particularly in the United States. The rise of self-help and personal development movements during the 1950s and 1960s created a fertile ground for numerology to thrive. Books on numerology became more widely available, and the practice began to be seen as a tool for personal empowerment and self-discovery.

Florence Campbell, another key figure in this era, authored *Your Days Are Numbered* (1931), which became a popular guide to understanding personal numerology. Her work emphasized the practical applications of numerology in everyday life, from understanding relationships to making career decisions. Campbell's accessible approach to numerology helped to demystify the practice and brought it to a wider audience.

1960 – 1980 CE – The New Age Movement and the Expansion of Numerology

The 1960s and 1970s were marked by the rise of the New Age movement, which embraced a wide range of spiritual and metaphysical practices, including numerology. During this time, numerology gained popularity as part of a broader interest in astrology, meditation, and holistic healing. The New Age movement's emphasis on personal transformation and spiritual growth resonated with the core principles of numerology, making it a natural fit.

During this period, many numerology books and courses were published, further expanding the practice. One of the most influential numerologists of this time was Dr. David A. Phillips, who authored *The Complete Book of Numerology* (1980). His work introduced a new generation to the concept of numerology, focusing on how numbers could reveal insights about personality, life purpose, and karmic patterns. Phillips' work is still widely used today and is considered a foundational text in modern numerology.

1980 – 2000 CE – Numerology in the Digital Age

The late 20th century saw the integration of numerology into the digital age. With the advent of personal computers and the internet, numerology became more accessible to the general public. Software programs and online calculators allowed individuals to easily generate their numerology charts, making the practice more user-friendly and popular than ever before.

The rise of the internet also facilitated the spread of numerological knowledge through websites, forums, and online communities. Numerology began to be featured in mainstream media, including magazines, newspapers, and television shows, further embedding it in popular culture. The accessibility and ease of use provided by digital tools helped to solidify numerology's place in the broader landscape of personal development and spirituality.

2000 – Present Day – The Globalization and Diversification of Numerology

In the 21st century, numerology has continued to grow in popularity, becoming a global phenomenon. The practice has diversified, with different schools of thought and variations emerging around the world. For example, while Western numerology remains dominant, other traditions like Vedic numerology from India and Chinese numerology have also gained recognition and are practiced widely.

Social media platforms have played a significant role in the resurgence of interest in numerology, with influencers, spiritual coaches, and content creators sharing numerological insights with millions of followers. This period has also seen the integration of numerology with other modern spiritual practices, such as manifestation techniques, mindfulness, and personal branding.

Moreover, the application of numerology has expanded into new areas, including business consulting, where companies use numerological analysis to choose names, logos, and even optimal dates for launching products. Numerology is also increasingly used in therapy and coaching, where it serves as a tool for understanding clients' underlying motivations and guiding them toward self-awareness and growth.

The widespread availability of information and the global interconnectedness provided by the internet have allowed numerology to adapt to contemporary needs, making it a versatile tool for self-discovery, spiritual growth, and practical decision-making in the modern world.

This timeline from 1900 to the present day highlights the evolution of numerology from its early modern roots to its current status as a widely recognized and practiced spiritual discipline. Numerology has shown a remarkable ability to adapt and grow, remaining relevant across different eras and cultures, and continuing to provide insights and guidance to those who seek to understand the deeper meanings behind numbers.

APPENDIX

Terms and Definitions

These terms cover the broad spectrum of concepts and practices within numerology, offering a comprehensive overview of how numbers influence different aspects of life and spirituality.

1. **Numerology**: The study of the mystical significance of numbers and their influence on human life and events.
2. **Life Path Number**: A core number in numerology calculated from the birth date, representing a person's life purpose and destiny.
3. **Expression Number**: Also known as the Destiny Number, it is derived from the full birth name and reflects natural talents and abilities.
4. **Soul Urge Number**: Also known as the Heart's Desire Number, it reveals a person's inner motivations and what they deeply desire.
5. **Personality Number**: Calculated from the consonants in a person's full name, it represents how others perceive them and their outward behavior.
6. **Birthday Number**: Derived from the day of birth, it provides insights into talents and potential challenges.
7. **Karmic Debt Number**: Indicates lessons that need to be learned in this lifetime, associated with challenges carried over from past lives.
8. **Master Numbers**: Powerful numbers in numerology, such as 11, 22, and 33, which carry higher spiritual significance and potential.
9. **Personal Year Number**: Indicates the theme and energy of a specific year in a person's life, guiding personal growth and opportunities.
10. **Personal Month Number**: Reflects the energy and opportunities available during a specific month, helping with short-term planning.
11. **Personal Day Number**: Offers insights into the daily energy and best actions to take on a specific day.
12. **Pythagorean Numerology**: The most common form of numerology, based on the teachings of Pythagoras, where each letter is assigned a number from 1 to 9.
13. **Chaldean Numerology**: An ancient system of numerology that assigns different numerical values to the alphabet, focusing on the name's vibrational energy.
14. **Kabbalistic Numerology**: A form of numerology derived from Jewish mysticism, using Hebrew letters and numbers to explore spiritual meanings.
15. **Vedic Numerology**: A numerology system from India, closely related to astrology, focusing on planetary influences on numbers.
16. **Gematria**: A method of interpreting Hebrew scriptures by assigning numerical values to letters and finding hidden meanings in the text.
17. **Core Numbers**: The main numbers in a numerology chart, including the Life Path, Expression, Soul Urge, Personality, and Birthday Numbers.

18. **Vibration**: The energy or frequency associated with a specific number, influencing personality traits and life events.
19. **Numerological Chart**: A chart that displays all of a person's core numbers, providing a comprehensive view of their numerological profile.
20. **Compatibility**: The degree to which two people's numerological charts align, indicating potential harmony or conflict in relationships.
21. **Cycles**: Refers to the different periods in a person's life, each influenced by specific numbers that guide growth and development.
22. **Pinnacle Numbers**: Four key numbers in a numerology chart that represent the four major phases of a person's life.
23. **Challenge Numbers**: Numbers that indicate the obstacles or challenges a person will face during the four Pinnacle phases.
24. **Essence Number**: Represents the theme and energy of a specific year, guiding a person's focus and actions during that time.
25. **Expression**: The way a person naturally expresses themselves, often revealed by the Expression Number.
26. **Triad Numbers**: Numbers that reflect different aspects of a person's life, including the Physical, Mental, and Spiritual Triads.
27. **Destiny Number**: Another term for the Expression Number, representing a person's life purpose and potential.
28. **Inner Dream Number**: Reflects hidden desires and what a person secretly dreams of achieving.
29. **Cornerstone**: The first letter of a person's name, indicating the foundation of their character and approach to life.
30. **Capstone**: The last letter of a person's name, representing how they finish tasks and their approach to endings.
31. **Heart's Desire**: Another term for the Soul Urge Number, revealing deep motivations and inner desires.
32. **Subconscious Self Number**: Reflects how a person responds to challenges and their level of self-awareness.
33. **Hidden Passion Number**: Indicates a dominant talent or passion that influences a person's life and choices.
34. **Balance Number**: Helps a person find balance in their life, especially during times of stress or conflict.
35. **Maturity Number**: Represents the ultimate goal or purpose that a person is meant to achieve later in life.
36. **Rational Thought Number**: Indicates a person's logical thinking process and how they approach problem-solving.
37. **Cornerstone Number**: Derived from the first letter of a person's name, reflecting their approach to life's challenges.
38. **Growth Number**: Suggests the areas in which a person is likely to experience the most growth and development.
39. **Day Number**: Derived from the day of birth, providing insights into specific talents and abilities.
40. **Quintessence Number**: Reflects the essence or core of a person's being, combining different aspects of their numerological chart.
41. **Universal Year Number**: Reflects the global energy of a specific year, influencing collective experiences and events.

42. **Universal Month Number**: Indicates the global energy of a specific month, influencing the collective mood and activities.
43. **Universal Day Number**: Reflects the global energy of a specific day, influencing worldwide events and decisions.
44. **Soul Path Number**: Indicates the spiritual path or journey that a person is meant to follow in this lifetime.
45. **Expression Cycle**: Refers to the different phases in a person's life, each influenced by their Expression Number.
46. **Destiny Cycle**: Represents the long-term themes and goals a person is meant to pursue, guided by their Destiny Number.
47. **Personal Year Cycle**: A cycle that repeats every nine years, influencing the themes and focus of each year in a person's life.
48. **Personal Month Cycle**: A monthly cycle that influences the opportunities and challenges a person will face.
49. **Personal Day Cycle**: A daily cycle that affects the energy and focus of each day, guiding daily decisions and actions.
50. **Master Number 11**: A Master Number associated with intuition, spiritual insight, and illumination.
51. **Master Number 22**: Known as the "Master Builder," this number is associated with practical wisdom, leadership, and the ability to turn dreams into reality.
52. **Master Number 33**: Known as the "Master Teacher," this number is associated with compassion, guidance, and selfless service to others.
53. **Physical Plane**: Refers to the material and physical aspects of life, often associated with numbers that reflect stability and practicality.
54. **Mental Plane**: Represents the intellectual and mental aspects of life, often associated with numbers that reflect logic and reasoning.
55. **Emotional Plane**: Refers to the emotional and relational aspects of life, often associated with numbers that reflect sensitivity and empathy.
56. **Spiritual Plane**: Represents the spiritual and metaphysical aspects of life, often associated with numbers that reflect intuition and higher consciousness.
57. **Name Number**: The numerical value derived from a person's name, reflecting their personality and life path.
58. **Birthday**: The specific day a person is born, which influences their character and life purpose.
59. **Signature Number**: Derived from a person's signature, reflecting their public persona and how they are perceived by others.
60. **Transit Numbers**: Numbers that influence a person during specific periods, reflecting the changing themes and energies in their life.
61. **Essence Cycle**: A cycle that reflects the underlying energy of a specific period, guiding personal growth and development.
62. **Peak Cycle**: Represents the most significant and influential period in a person's life, often marked by major achievements or challenges.
63. **Minor Challenge Number**: Indicates temporary challenges or obstacles that may arise during specific periods.
64. **Major Challenge Number**: Reflects long-term challenges that shape a person's life and character.

65. **Ascendant Number**: Represents the external energy that influences a person's interactions with the world.
66. **Mundane Numerology**: Refers to the study of numerology as it applies to worldly events, including politics, economics, and social trends.
67. **Numerological Grid**: A chart that displays the numbers associated with a person's name and birth date, used to analyze their numerological profile.
68. **Numerological Reduction**: The process of reducing multi-digit numbers to a single digit (or Master Number) to uncover their core significance.
69. **Soul Plane**: Refers to the aspects of life that relate to a person's inner spiritual essence, often connected with higher consciousness and purpose.
70. **Numeroscope**: A numerological chart or diagram that visually represents a person's key numbers, similar to a horoscope in astrology.
71. **Compound Number**: A number that is not reduced to a single digit in numerology, often analyzed for its unique vibrational meaning before reduction.
72. **Numerological Forecasting**: The practice of predicting future trends or events in a person's life based on their numerological chart and cycles.
73. **Energy Alignment**: The process of harmonizing one's actions and decisions with the vibrations of their numerological numbers to achieve balance and success.
74. **Numerological Compatibility**: The degree to which two or more people's numerological charts align, influencing their relationships and interactions.
75. **Numerical Symmetry**: The occurrence of repeating or mirrored numbers in a numerological chart, often indicating harmony or balance.
76. **Spiritual Number**: A number in a numerology chart that has a strong connection to spiritual growth and enlightenment, such as the Master Numbers.
77. **Numerological Affirmations**: Positive statements or mantras that are created based on a person's numerology, intended to align their thoughts with their life path or goals.
78. **Numerological Timing**: The practice of choosing the best times for actions or decisions based on the numerological energy of specific dates or periods.
79. **Ascension Number**: A term used to describe a number that represents a person's spiritual evolution or journey toward higher consciousness.
80. **Numerological Archetypes**: The symbolic representations of numbers, where each number embodies specific traits, energies, or life lessons.
81. **Numerical Patterns**: Recurring sequences of numbers that appear in a person's life, often seen as messages or signs from the universe.
82. **Numerological Influences**: The impact that a person's core numbers have on their personality, behavior, and life experiences.
83. **Numerology Matrix**: A comprehensive grid or table that organizes all of a person's key numbers and their interactions, used for in-depth analysis.

AFTERWORD

As you reach the end of this journey through the study of Numerology, I hope you've gained a deeper understanding and appreciation for the profound impact that numbers can have on our lives. Whether you've been a lifelong numerology enthusiast or this is your first introduction to the subject, I trust that the insights and techniques you've learned will serve you well in the years to come.

Throughout this book, we've explored the various facets of numerology, from the core principles to the intricacies of personal numbers, compatibility, and even advanced applications. You now have the knowledge and concepts to interpret your own numerology chart and apply these insights to your daily life.

But the true power of numerology lies not just in the numbers themselves, but in how we choose to use that knowledge to create positive change. Numerology is not a rigid system, but a dynamic framework for self-discovery, personal growth, and spiritual evolution.

As you continue your numerology journey, I encourage you to approach it with an open mind and a willingness to explore. Use the information in this book as a starting point, but don't be afraid to go deeper, experiment, and find your own unique way of integrating numerology into your life.

The numbers in your life are not just random occurrences – they are signposts, guiding you towards your highest potential. By understanding and embracing these numbers, you can make more informed decisions, strengthen your relationships, and unlock the hidden talents and abilities that have been waiting to be discovered.

So, as you close this book and step out into the world, I invite you to continue your exploration of numerology. Observe the patterns and synchronicities in your life, and use your newfound knowledge to navigate the challenges and opportunities that come your way.

Embrace the power of numbers, trust your intuition, and never stop learning and growing. The journey of self-discovery is an ongoing one, but with the guidance of numerology, you'll be equipped to take on whatever life has in store.

Printed in Great Britain
by Amazon